THE

CHIMNEY-CORNER.

D1498191

THE

CHIMNEY-CORNER.

BY

HARRIET BEECHER STOWE
(Christopher Crowfield)

Essay Index Reprint Series

BOOKS FOR LIBRARIES PRESS
PLAINVIEW, NEW YORK

First Published 1868
Reprinted 1972

Library of Congress Cataloging in Publication Data

Stowe, Harriet Elizabeth (Beecher) 1811-1896.
   The chimney-corner.

   (Essay index reprint series)
   Reprint of the 1868 ed.
   1. Woman--Social and moral questions. I. Title.
HQ1426.S85 1972   301.41'2   72-8589
ISBN 0-8369-7330-5

CONTENTS.

———

CONTENTS.

THE CHIMNEY-CORNER.

I.

WHAT WILL YOU DO WITH HER? OR, THE WOMAN QUESTION.

"WELL, what will you do with her?" said I to my wife.

My wife had just come down from an interview with a pale, faded-looking young woman in rusty black attire, who had called upon me on the very common supposition that I was an editor of the "Atlantic Monthly."

By the by, this is a mistake that brings me, Christopher Crowfield, many letters that do not belong to me, and which might with equal pertinency be addressed, "To the Man in the Moon." Yet these letters often make my heart ache, — they speak so of people who strive and sorrow and want help; and it is hard to be called on in plaintive tones for help which you know it is perfectly impossible for you to give.

For instance, you get a letter in a delicate hand,

setting forth the old distress, — she is poor, and she has looking to her for support those that are poorer and more helpless than herself: she has tried sewing, but can make little at it; tried teaching, but cannot now get a school, — all places being filled, and more than filled; at last has tried literature, and written some little things, of which she sends you a modest specimen, and wants your opinion whether she can gain her living by writing. You run over the articles, and perceive at a glance that there is no kind of hope or use in her trying to do anything at literature; and then you ask yourself, mentally, "What is to be done with her? What can she do?"

Such was the application that had come to me this morning, — only, instead of by note, it came, as I have said, in the person of the applicant, a thin, delicate, consumptive-looking being, wearing that rusty mourning which speaks sadly at once of heart-bereavement and material poverty.

My usual course is to turn such cases over to Mrs. Crowfield; and it is to be confessed that this worthy woman spends a large portion of her time, and wears out an extraordinary amount of shoe-leather, in performing the duties of a self-constituted intelligence-office.

Talk of giving money to the poor! what is that, compared to giving sympathy, thought, time, taking their burdens upon you, sharing their perplexities? They who are able to buy off every application at the door of their heart with a five or ten dollar bill are those who free themselves at least expense.

My wife had communicated to our friend, in the gentlest tones and in the blandest manner, that her poor little pieces, however interesting to her own household circle, had nothing in them wherewith to enable her to make her way in the thronged and crowded thoroughfare of letters, — that they had no more strength or adaptation to win bread for her than a broken-winged butterfly to draw a plough; and it took some resolution in the background of her tenderness to make the poor applicant entirely certain of this. In cases like this, absolute certainty is the very greatest, the only true kindness.

It was grievous, my wife said, to see the discouraged shade which passed over her thin, tremulous features, when this certainty forced itself upon her. It is hard, when sinking in the waves, to see the frail bush at which the hand clutches uprooted; hard, when alone in the crowded thoroughfare of travel, to have one's last bank-note declared a counterfeit. I knew I should not be able to see her face, under the shade of this disappointment; and so, coward that I was, I turned this trouble, where I have turned so many others, upon my wife.

"Well, what shall we do with her?" said I.

"I really don't know," said my wife, musingly.

"Do you think we could get that school in Taunton for her?"

"Impossible; Mr. Herbert told me he had already twelve applicants for it."

"Couldn't you get her plain sewing? Is she handy with her needle?"

"She has tried that, but it brings on a pain in her side, and cough; and the doctor has told her it will not do for her to confine herself."

"How is her handwriting? Does she write a good hand?"

"Only passable."

"Because," said I, "I was thinking if I could get Steele and Simpson to give her law-papers to copy."

"They have more copyists than they need now; and, in fact, this woman does not write the sort of hand at all that would enable her to get on as a copyist."

"Well," said I, turning uneasily in my chair, and at last hitting on a bright masculine expedient, "I'll tell you what must be done. She must get married."

"My dear," said my wife, "marrying for a living is the very hardest way a woman can take to get it. Even marrying for love often turns out badly enough. Witness poor Jane."

Jane was one of the large number of people whom it seemed my wife's fortune to carry through life on her back. She was a pretty, smiling, pleasing daughter of Erin, who had been in our family originally as nursery-maid. I had been greatly pleased in watching a little idyllic affair growing up between her and a joyous, good-natured young Irishman, to whom at last we married her. Mike soon after, however, took to drinking and unsteady courses; and the result has been to Jane only a yearly baby, with poor health, and no money.

"In fact," said my wife, "if Jane had only kept single, she could have made her own way well enough, and might have now been in good health and had a pretty sum in the savings bank. As it is, I must carry not only her, but her three children, on my back."

"You ought to drop her, my dear. You really ought not to burden yourself with other people's affairs as you do," said I, inconsistently.

"How *can* I drop her? Can I help knowing that she is poor and suffering? And if I drop her, who will take her up?"

Now there is a way of getting rid of cases of this kind, spoken of in a quaint old book, which occurred strongly to me at this moment :—

"If a brother or sister be naked, and destitute of daily food, and one of you say unto them, 'Depart in peace, be ye warmed and filled,' notwithstanding ye give them not those things which are needful to the body. what doth it profit?"

I must confess, notwithstanding the strong point of the closing question, I looked with an evil eye of longing on this very easy way of disposing of such cases. A few sympathizing words, a few expressions of hope that I did not feel, a line written to turn the case into somebody else's hands, — any expedient, in fact, to hide the longing eyes and imploring hands from my sight, was what my carnal nature at this moment greatly craved.

"Besides," said my wife, resuming the thread of her thoughts in regard to the subject just now before us, "as to marriage, it's out of the question at present for this poor child; for the man she loved and would have married lies low in one of the graves before Richmond. It's a sad story, — one of a thousand like it. She brightened for a few moments, and looked almost handsome, when she spoke of his bravery and goodness. Her father and lover have both died in this war. Her only brother has returned from it a broken-down cripple, and she has him and her poor old mother to care for, and so she seeks work. I told her to come again to-morrow, and I would look about for her a little to-day."

"Let me see, how many are now down on your

list to be looked about for, Mrs. Crowfield? — some
twelve or thirteen, are there not? You've got Tom's
sister disposed of finally, I hope, — that's a comfort!"

"Well, I'm sorry to say she came back on my hands
yesterday," said my wife, patiently. "She is a foolish
young thing, and said she did n't like living out in the
country. I'm sorry, because the Morrises are an
excellent family, and she might have had a life-home
there, if she had only been steady, and chosen to
behave herself properly. But yesterday I found her
back on her mother's hands again; and the poor
woman told me that the dear child never could bear
to be separated from her, and that she had n't the
heart to send her back."

"And in short," said I, "she gave you notice that
you must provide for Miss O'Connor in some more
agreeable way. Cross that name off your list, at any
rate. That woman and girl need a few hard raps in
the school of experience before you can do anything
for them."

"I think I shall," said my long-suffering wife; "but
it's a pity to see a young thing put in the direct road
to ruin."

"It is one of the inevitables," said I, "and we
must save our strength for those that are willing to
help themselves."

"What's all this talk about?" said Bob, coming in upon us rather brusquely.

"O, as usual, the old question," said I, — "'What's to be done with her?'"

"Well," said Bob, "it's exactly what I've come to talk with mother about. Since she keeps a distressed-women's agency-office, I've come to consult her about Marianne. That woman will die before six months are out, a victim to high civilization and the Paddies. There we are, twelve miles out from Boston, in a country villa so convenient that every part of it might almost do its own work, — everything arranged in the most convenient, contiguous, self-adjusting, self-acting, patent-right, perfective manner, — and yet, I tell you, Marianne will die of that house. It will yet be recorded on her tombstone, 'Died of conveniences.' For myself, what I languish for is a log cabin, with a bed in one corner, a trundle-bed underneath for the children, a fireplace only six feet off, a table, four chairs, one kettle, a coffee-pot, and a tin baker, — that's all. I lived deliciously in an establishment of this kind last summer, when I was up at Lake Superior; and I am convinced, if I could move Marianne into it at once, that she would become a healthy and a happy woman. Her life is smothered out of her with comforts; we have too many rooms, too many carpets, too many vases and knick-knacks, too much china and silver ; she has too many laces and dresses and bonnets; the children all have too many clothes ; — in fact, to put it scripturally, our riches are corrupted, our garments are moth-eaten, our gold and our silver is cankered,— and, in short, Marianne is sick in bed, and I have come to the agency-office-for-distressed-women to take you out to attend to her.

" The fact is," continued Bob, "that since our cook married, and Alice went to California, there seems to be no possibility of putting our domestic cabinet upon any permanent basis. The number of female persons that have been through our house, and the ravages they have wrought on it for the last six' months, pass belief. I had yesterday a bill of sixty dollars' plumbing to pay for damages of various kinds which had had to be repaired in our very convenient water-works ; and the blame of each particular one had been bandied like a shuttlecock among our three household divinities. Biddy privately assured my wife that Kate was in the habit of emptying dust-pans of rubbish into the main drain from the chambers, and washing any little extra bits down through the bowls ; and, in fact, when one of the bathing-room bowls had overflowed so as to damage the frescoes below, my wife, with great delicacy and precaution, interrogated Kate as to whether she had followed her instructions in the care of the water pipes. Of course she protested the most immaculate

I *

care and circumspection. 'Sure, and she knew how careful one ought to be, and wasn't of the likes of thim as wouldn't mind what throuble they made, — like Biddy, who would throw trash and hair in the pipes, and niver listen to her tellin'; sure, and hadn't she broken the pipes in the kitchen, and lost the stoppers, as it was a shame to see in a Christian house?' Ann, the third girl, being privately questioned, blamed Biddy on Monday, and Kate on Tuesday; on Wednesday, however, she exonerated both; but on Thursday, being in a high quarrel with both, she departed, accusing them severally, not only of all the evil practices aforesaid, but of lying, and stealing, and all other miscellaneous wickednesses that came to hand. Whereat the two thus accused rushed in, bewailing themselves and cursing Ann in alternate strophes, averring that she had given the baby laudanum, and, taking it out riding, had stopped for hours with it in a filthy lane, where the scarlet fever was said to be rife, — in short, made so fearful a picture, that Marianne gave up the child's life at once, and has taken to her bed. I have endeavored all I could to quiet her, by telling her that the scarlet-fever story was probably an extemporaneous work of fiction, got up to gratify the Hibernian anger at Ann; and that it wasn't in the least worth while to believe one thing more than another from the fact that any of the tribe said it. But she refuses to be comforted, and

is so Utopian as to lie there, crying, ' O, if I only
could get one that I could trust, — one that really would
speak the truth to me, — one that I might know really
went where she said she went, and really did as she
said she did ! ' To have to live so, she says, and bring
up little children with those she can't trust out of her
sight, whose word is good for nothing, — to feel that her
beautiful house and her lovely things are all going to
rack and ruin, and she can't take care of them, and
can't see where or when or how the mischief is done, —
in short, the poor child talks as women do who are
violently attacked with housekeeping fever tending to
congestion of the brain. She actually yesterday told
me that she wished, on the whole, she never had got
married, which I take to be the most positive indication of mental alienation."

" Here," said I, " we behold at this moment two
women dying for the want of what they can mutually
give one another, — each having a supply of what the
other needs, but held back by certain invisible cob-
webs, slight but strong, from coming to each other's
assistance. Marianne has money enough, but she
wants a helper in her family, such as all her money
has been hitherto unable to buy ; and here, close at
hand, is a woman who wants home-shelter, healthy, varied, active, cheerful labor, with nourishing food, kind
care, and good wages. What hinders these women

from rushing to the help of one another, just as two drops of water on a leaf rush together and make one? Nothing but a miserable prejudice, — but a prejudice so strong that women will starve in any other mode of life, rather than accept competency and comfort in this."

"You don't mean," said my wife, "to propose that our *protégée* should go to Marianne as a servant?"

"I do say it would be the best thing for her to do, — the only opening that I see, and a very good one, too, it is. Just look at it. Her bare living at this moment cannot cost her less than five or six dollars a week, — everything at the present time is so very dear in the city. Now by what possible calling open to her capacity can she pay her board and washing, fuel and lights, and clear a hundred and some odd dollars a year? She could not do it as a district school-teacher; she certainly cannot, with her feeble health, do it by plain sewing; she could not do it as a copyist. A robust woman might go into a factory, and earn more; but factory work is unintermitted, twelve hours daily, week in and out, in the same movement, in close air, amid the clatter of machinery; and a person delicately organized soon sinks under it. It takes a stolid, enduring temperament to bear factory labor. Now look at Marianne's house and family, and see what is insured to your *protégée* there.

" In the first place, a home, — a neat, quiet chamber, quite as good as she has probably been accustomed to, — the very best of food, served in a pleasant,
light, airy kitchen, which is one of the most agreeable
rooms in the house, and the table and table-service
quite equal to those of most farmers and mechanics
Then her daily tasks would be light and varied, —
some sweeping, some dusting, the washing and dressing of children, the care of their rooms and the nursery, — all of it the most healthful, the most natural
work of a woman, — work alternating with rest, and
diverting thought from painful subjects by its variety,
— and what is more, a kind of work in which a good
Christian woman might have satisfaction, as feeling
herself useful in the highest and best way ; for the
child's nurse, if she be a pious, well-educated woman,
may make the whole course of nursery-life an education in goodness.   Then, what is far different from
many other modes of gaining a livelihood, a woman in
this capacity can make and feel herself really and
truly beloved.   The hearts of little children are easily
gained, and their love is real and warm, and no true
woman can become the object of it without feeling
her own life made brighter.   Again, she would have
in Marianne a sincere, warm - hearted friend, who
would care for her tenderly, respect her sorrows, shelter her feelings, be considerate of her wants, and in

every way aid her in the cause she has most at heart, — the succor of her family. There are many ways besides her wages in which she would infallibly be assisted by Marianne, so that the probability would be that she could send her little salary almost untouched to those for whose support she was toiling, — all this on her part."

"But," added my wife, "on the other hand, she would be obliged to associate and be ranked with common Irish servants."

"Well," I answered, "is there any occupation, by which any of us gain our living, which has not its disagreeable side? Does not the lawyer spend all his days either in a dusty office or in the foul air of a court-room? Is he not brought into much disagreeable contact with the lowest class of society? Are not his labors dry and hard and exhausting? Does not the blacksmith spend half his life in soot and grime, that he may gain a competence for the other half? If this woman were to work in a factory, would she not often be brought into associations distasteful to her? Might it not be the same in any of the arts and trades in which a living is to be got? There must be unpleasant circumstances about earning a living in any way; only I maintain that those which a woman would be likely to meet with as a servant in a refined, well-bred, Christian family would be less than in almost any other calling. Are there no trials to a woman, I beg to know, in teaching a district school, where all the boys, big and little, of a neighborhood congregate? For my part, were it my daughter or sister who was in necessitous circumstances, I would choose for her a position such as I name, in a kind, intelligent, Christian family, before many of those to which women do devote themselves."

"Well," said Bob, "all this has a good sound enough, but it's quite impossible. It's true, I verily believe, that such a kind of servant in our family would really prolong Marianne's life years, — that it would improve her health, and be an unspeakable blessing to her, to me, and the children, — and I would almost go down on my knees to a really well-educated, good, American woman who would come into our family, and take that place ; but I know it's perfectly vain and useless to expect it. You know we have tried the experiment two or three times of having a person in our family who should be on the footing of a friend, yet do the duties of a servant, and that we *never* could make it work well. These half-and-half people are so sensitive, so exacting in their demands, so hard to please, that we have come to the firm determination that we will have no sliding-scale in our family, and that whoever we are to depend on must come with *bona-fide* willingness to take the position of a servant, such as that position is in our house; and *that,* I suppose, your *protégée* would never do, even if she could thereby live easier, have less hard work, better health, and quite as much money as she could earn in any other way."

"She would consider it a personal degradation, I suppose," said my wife.

"And yet, if she only knew it," said Bob, "I should respect her far more profoundly for her willingness to take that position, when adverse fortune has shut other doors."

"Well, now," said I, "this woman is, as I understand, the daughter of a respectable stone-mason; and the domestic habits of her early life have probably been economical and simple. Like most of our mechanics' daughters, she has received in one of our high schools an education which has cultivated and developed her mind far beyond those of her parents and the associates of her childhood. This is a common fact in our American life. By our high schools the daughters of plain workingmen are raised to a state of intellectual culture which seems to make the disposition of them in any kind of industrial calling a difficult one. They all want to teach school, — and school-teaching, consequently, is an overcrowded profession, — and, failing that, there is only millinery and dressmaking. Of late, it is true, efforts have been

made in various directions to widen their sphere.
Type-setting and book-keeping are in some instances
beginning to be open to them.

"All this time there is lying, neglected and de-
spised, a calling to which womanly talents and instincts are peculiarly fitted, — a calling full of opportunities of the most lasting usefulness, — a calling
which insures a settled home, respectable protection,
healthful exercise, good air, good food, and good
wages, — a calling in which a woman may make real
friends, and secure to herself warm affection ; and yet
this calling is the one always refused, shunned, con-
temned, left to the alien and the stranger, and that
simply and solely because it bears the name of *servant.*
A Christian woman, who holds the name of Christ in
her heart in true devotion, would think it the greatest
possible misfortune and degradation to become like
him in taking upon her 'the form of a servant.' The
founder of Christianity says, 'Whether is greater, he
that sitteth at meat or he that serveth? But *I* am
among you as he that serveth.' But notwithstanding
these so plain declarations of Jesus, we find that
scarce any one in a Christian land will accept real
advantages of position and employment that come
with that name and condition."

"I suppose," said my wife, "I could prevail upon
this woman to do all the duties of the situation, if she

B

could be, as they phrase it, 'treated as one of the family.'"

"That is to say," said Bob, "if she could sit with us at the same table, be introduced to our friends, and be in all respects as one of us. Now as to this, I am free to say that I have no false aristocratic scruples. I consider every well-educated woman as fully my equal, not to say my superior; but it does not follow from this that she would be one whom I should wish to make a third party with me and my wife at meal-times. Our meals are often our seasons of privacy, — the times when we wish in perfect unreserve to speak of matters that concern ourselves and our family alone. Even invited guests and family friends would not be always welcome, however agreeable at times. Now a woman may be perfectly worthy of respect, and we may be perfectly respectful to her, whom nevertheless we do not wish to take into the circle of intimate friendship. I regard the position of a woman who comes to perform domestic service as I do any other business relation. We have a very respectable young lady in our employ, who does legal copying for us, and all is perfectly pleasant and agreeable in our mutual relations; but the case would be far otherwise, were she to take it into her head that we treated her with contempt, because my wife did not call on her, and because she was not occasionally invited to tea. Besides, I apprehend that a woman of quick sensibilities, employed in domestic service, and who was so far treated as a member of the family as to share our table, would find her position even more painful and embarrassing than if she took once for all the position of a servant. We could not control the feelings of our friends; we could not always insure that they would be free from aristocratic prejudice, even were we so ourselves. We could not force her upon their acquaintance, and she might feel far more slighted than she would in a position where no attentions of any kind were to be expected. Besides which, I have always noticed that persons standing in this uncertain position are objects of peculiar antipathy to the servants in full; that they are the cause of constant and secret cabals and discontents; and that a family where the two orders exist has always raked up in it the smouldering embers of a quarrel ready at any time to burst out into open feud."

"Well," said I, " here lies the problem of American life. Half our women, like Marianne, are being faded and made old before their time by exhausting endeavors to lead a life of high civilization and refinement with only such untrained help as is washed up on our shores by the tide of emigration. Our houses are built upon a plan that precludes the necessity of much hard labor, but requires rather careful and nice handling. A well-trained, intelligent woman, who had vitalized her finger-ends by means of a well-developed brain, could do all the work of such a house with comparatively little physical fatigue. So stands the case as regards our houses. Now over against the women that are perishing in them from too much care, there is another class of American women that are wandering up and down, perishing for lack of some remunerating employment. That class of women, whose developed brains and less developed muscles mark them as peculiarly fitted for the performance of the labors of a high civilization, stand utterly aloof from paid domestic service. Sooner beg, sooner starve, sooner marry for money, sooner hang on as dependants in families where they know they are not wanted, than accept of a quiet home, easy, healthful work, and certain wages, in these refined and pleasant modern dwellings of ours."

" What is the reason of this ? " said Bob.

" The reason is, that we have not yet come to the full development of Christian democracy. The taint of old aristocracies is yet pervading all parts of our society. We have not yet realized fully the true dignity of labor, and the surpassing dignity of domestic labor. And I must say that the valuable and coura-geous women who have agitated the doctrines of Woman's Rights among us have not in all things seen their way clear in this matter."

"Don't talk to me of those creatures," said Bob, "those men-women, those anomalies, neither flesh nor fish, with their conventions, and their cracked woman-voices strained in what they call public speaking, but which I call public squeaking! No man reverences true women more than I do. I hold a real, true, thoroughly good *woman*, whether in my parlor or my kitchen, as my superior. She can always teach me something that I need to know. She has always in her somewhat of the divine gift of prophecy; but in order to keep it, she must remain a woman. When she crops her hair, puts on pantaloons, and strides about in conventions, she is an abortion, and not a woman."

"Come! come!" said I, "after all, speak with deference. We that choose to wear soft clothing and dwell in kings' houses must respect the Baptists, who wear leathern girdles, and eat locusts and wild honey. They are the voices crying in the wilderness, preparing the way for a coming good. They go down on their knees in the mire of life to lift up and brighten and restore a neglected truth; and we that have not the energy to share their struggle should at least refrain from criticising their soiled garments and ungraceful action. There have been excrescences, eccentricities, peculiarities, about the camp of these reformers; but the body of them have been true and noble women, and worthy of all the reverence due to such. They have already in many of our States reformed the laws relating to woman's position, and placed her on a more just and Christian basis. It is through their movements that in many of our States a woman can hold the fruits of her own earnings, if it be her ill luck to have a worthless, drunken spendthrift for a husband. It is owing to their exertions that new trades and professions are opening to woman; and all that I have to say of them is, that in the suddenness of their zeal for opening new paths for her feet, they have not sufficiently considered the propriety of straightening, widening, and mending the one broad, good old path of domestic labor, established by God himself. It does appear to me, that, if at least a portion of their zeal could be spent in removing the stones out of this highway of domestic life, and making it pleasant and honorable, they would effect even more. I would not have them leave undone what they are doing; but I would, were I worthy to be considered, humbly suggest to their prophetic wisdom and enthusiasm, whether, in this new future of women which they wish to introduce, women's natural, God - given employment of *domestic service* is not to receive a new character, and rise in a new form

"'To love and serve' is a motto worn with pride

on some aristocratic family shields in England. It ought to be graven on the Christian shield. *Servant* is the name which Christ gives to the *Christian;* and in speaking of his kingdom as distinguished from earthly kingdoms, he distinctly said, that rank there should be conditioned, not upon desire to command, but on willingness to serve.

" ' Ye know that the princes of the Gentiles exercise dominion over them, and they that are great exercise authority upon them. But it shall not be so among you : but whosoever will be great among you, let him be your minister ; and whosoever will be chief among you, let him be your *servant.*'

" Why is it, that this name of servant, which Christ says is the highest in the kingdom of heaven, is so dishonored among us professing Christians, that good women will beg or starve, will suffer almost any extreme of poverty and privation, rather than accept home, competence, security, with this honored name ? "

"The fault with many of our friends of the Woman's Rights order," said my wife, " is the depreciatory tone in which they have spoken of the domestic labors of a family as being altogether below the scope of the faculties of woman. *'Domestic drudgery'* they call it, — an expression that has done more harm than any two words that ever were put together.

" Think of a woman's calling clear-starching **and**

ironing domestic drudgery, and to better the matter turning to type-setting in a grimy printing-office! Call the care of china and silver, the sweeping of carpets, the arrangement of parlors and sitting-rooms, drudgery; and go into a factory and spend the day amid the whir and clatter and thunder of machinery, inhaling an atmosphere loaded with wool and machine-grease, and keeping on the feet for twelve hours, nearly continuously! Think of its being called drudgery to take care of a clean, light, airy nursery, to wash and dress and care for two or three children, to mend their clothes, tell them stories, make them playthings, take them out walking or driving; and rather than this, to wear out the whole livelong day, extending often deep into the night, in endless sewing, in a close room of a dressmaking establishment! Is it any less drudgery to stand all day behind a counter, serving customers, than to tend a door-bell and wait on a table? For my part," said my wife, "I have often thought the matter over, and concluded, that, if I were left in straitened circumstances, as many are in a great city, I would seek a position as a servant in one of our good families."

"I envy the family that you even think of in that connection," said I. "I fancy the amazement which would take possession of them as you began to develop among them."

"I have always held," said my wife, "that family work, in many of its branches, can be better performed by an educated woman than an uneducated one. Just as an army where even the bayonets think is superior to one of mere brute force and mechanical training, so, I have heard it said, some of our distinguished modern female reformers show an equal superiority in the domestic sphere, — and I do not doubt it. Family work was never meant to be the special province of untaught brains. I have sometimes thought I should like to show what I could do as a servant."

"Well," said Bob, "to return from all this to the question, What's to be done with her? Are you going to *my* distressed woman? If you are, suppose you take *your* distressed woman along, and ask her to try it. I can promise her a pleasant house, a quiet room by herself, healthful and not too hard work, a kind friend, and some leisure for reading, writing, or whatever other pursuit of her own she may choose for her recreation. We are always quite willing to lend books to any who appreciate them. Our house is surrounded by pleasant grounds, which are open to our servants as to ourselves. So let her come and try us. I am quite sure that country air, quiet security, and moderate exercise in a good home, will bring up her health; and if she is willing to take the one or two disagreeables which may come with all this, let her try us."

"Well," said I, "so be it; and would that all the women seeking homes and employment could thus fall in with women who have homes and are perishing in them for want of educated helpers!"

On this question of woman's work I have yet more to say, but must defer it till another time.

II.

WOMAN'S SPHERE.

"WHAT do you think of this Woman's Rights question?" said Bob Stephens. "From some of your remarks, I apprehend that you think there is something in it. I may be wrong, but I must confess that I have looked with disgust on the whole movement. No man reverences women as I do; but I reverence them *as* women. I reverence them for those very things in which their sex differs from ours; but when they come upon our ground, and begin to work and fight after our manner and with our weapons, I regard them as fearful anomalies, neither men nor women. These Woman's Rights Conventions appear to me to have ventilated crudities, absurdities, and blasphemies. To hear them talk about men, one would suppose that the two sexes were natural-born enemies, and wonders whether they ever had fathers and brothers. One would think, upon their showing, that all men were a set of ruffians, in league against

women, — they seeming, at the same time, to forget
how on their very platforms the most constant and
gallant defenders of their rights are men.   Wendell
Phillips and Wentworth Higginson have put at the
service of the cause masculine training and manly
vehemence, and complacently accepted the wholesale
abuse of their own sex at the hands of their warrior
sisters.   One would think, were all they say of female
powers true, that our Joan-of-Arcs ought to have dis-
dained to fight under male captains."

"I think," said my wife, "that, in all this talk about
the rights of men, and the rights of women, and the
rights of children, the world seems to be forgetting
what is quite as important, the *duties* of men and
women and children.   We all hear of our *rights* till
we forget our *duties ;* and even theology is beginning
to concern itself more with what man has a right to
expect of his Creator than what the Creator has a
right to expect of man."

"You say the truth," said I ; "there is danger of
just this overaction ; and yet rights must be discussed ; because, in order to understand the duties we
owe to any class, we must understand their rights.   To
know our duties to men, women, and children, we must
know what the rights of men, women, and children
justly are.   As to the ' Woman's Rights movement,' it
is not peculiar to America, it is part of a great wave

in the incoming tide of modern civilization ; the swell
is felt no less in Europe, but it combs over and breaks
on our American shore, because our great wide beach
affords the best play for its waters ; and as the ocean
waves bring with them kelp, sea-weed, mud, sand,
gravel, and even putrefying debris, which lie unsightly
on the shore, and yet, on the whole, are healthful and
refreshing, — so the Woman's Rights movement, with
its conventions, its speech-makings, its crudities, and
eccentricities, is nevertheless a part of a healthful and
necessary movement of the human race towards progress. This question of Woman and her Sphere is now,
perhaps, the greatest of the age. We have put Slavery
under foot, and with the downfall of Slavery the only
obstacle to the success of our great democratic experiment is overthrown, and there seems no limit to the
splendid possibilities which it may open before the
human race.

"In the reconstruction that is now coming there
lies more than the reconstruction of States and the
arrangement of the machinery of government. We
need to know and feel, all of us, that, from the moment of the death of Slavery, we parted finally from
the *régime* and control of all the old ideas formed
under old oppressive systems of society, and came
upon a new plane of life.

"In this new life we must never forget that we are a

peculiar people, that we have to walk in paths unknown to the Old World, -- paths where its wisdom cannot guide us, where its precedents can be of little use to us, and its criticisms, in most cases, must be wholly irrelevant. The history of our war has shown us of how little service to us in any important crisis the opinions and advice of the Old World can be. We have been hurt at what seemed to us the want of sympathy, the direct antagonism, of England. We might have been less hurt if we had properly understood that Providence had placed us in a position so far ahead of her ideas or power of comprehension, that just judgment or sympathy was not to be expected from her.

" As we went through our great war with no help but that of God, obliged to disregard the misconceptions and impertinences which the foreign press rained down upon us, so, if we are wise, we shall continue to do. Our object must now be to make the principles on which our government is founded permeate consistently the mass of society, and to purge out the leaven of aristocratic and Old World ideas. So long as there is an illogical working in our actual life, so long as there is any class denied equal rights with other classes, so long will there be agitation and trouble."

" Then," said my wife, " you believe that women ought to vote?"

" If the principle on which we founded our government is true, that taxation must not exist without representation, and if women hold property and are taxed, it follows that women should be represented in the State by their votes, or there is an illogical working of our government."

"But, my dear, don't you think that this will have a bad effect on the female character?"

"Yes," said Bob, "it will make women caucus-holders, political candidates."

"It may make this of some women, just as of some men," said I. "But all men do not take any great interest in politics; it is very difficult to get some of the best of them to do their duty in voting; and the same will be found true among women."

"But, after all," said Bob, "what do you gain? What will a woman's vote be but a duplicate of that of her husband or father, or whatever man happens to be her adviser?"

"That may be true on a variety of questions; but there are subjects on which the vote of women would, I think, be essentially different from that of men. On the subjects of temperance, public morals, and education, I have no doubt that the introduction of the female vote into legislation, in States, counties, and cities, would produce results very different from that of men alone. There are thousands of women who would close grogshops, and stop the traffic in spirits, if they had the legislative power; and it would be well for society if they had. In fact, I think that a State can no more afford to dispense with the vote of women in its affairs than a family. Imagine a family where the female has no voice in the housekeeping! A State is but a larger family, and there are many of its concerns which equally with those of a private household would be bettered by female supervision."

"But fancy women going to those horrible voting-places! It is more than I can do myself," said Bob.

"But you forget," said I, "that they are horrible and disgusting principally because women never go to them. All places where women are excluded tend downward to barbarism; but the moment she is introduced, there come in with her courtesy, cleanliness, sobriety, and order. When a man can walk up to the ballot-box with his wife or his sister on his arm, voting-places will be far more agreeable than now; and the polls will not be such bear-gardens that refined men will be constantly tempted to omit their political duties there.

"If for nothing else, I would have women vote, that the business of voting may not be so disagreeable and intolerable to men of refinement as it now is; and I sincerely believe that the cause of good morals, good order, cleanliness, and public health would be a gainer not merely by the added feminine vote, but by the added vote of a great many excellent, but too fastidious men, who are now kept from the polls by the disagreeables they meet there.

"Do you suppose, that, if women had equal representation with men in the municipal laws of New York, its reputation for filth during the last year would have gone so far beyond that of Cologne, or any other city renowned for bad smells? I trow not. I believe a *lady-mayoress* would have brought in a dispensation of brooms and whitewash, and made a terrible searching into dark holes and vile corners, before now. *Female* New York, I have faith to believe, has yet left in her enough of the primary instincts of womanhood to give us a clean, healthy city, if female votes had any power to do it."

"But," said Bob, "you forget that voting would bring together all the women of the lower classes."

"Yes; but thanks to the instincts of their sex, they would come in their Sunday clothes; for where is the woman that has n't her finery, and will not embrace every chance to show it? Biddy's parasol, and hat with pink ribbons, would necessitate a clean shirt in Pat as much as on Sunday. Voting would become a *fête*, and we should have a population at the polls as well dressed as at church. Such is my belief."

"I do not see," said Bob, "but you go to the full extent with our modern female reformers."

" There are certain neglected truths, which have been held up by these reformers, that are gradually being accepted and infused into the life of modern society ; and their recognition will help to solidify and purify democratic institutions. They are, —

" 1. The right of every woman to hold independent property.

" 2. The right of every woman to receive equal pay with man for work which she does equally well.

" 3. The right of any woman to do any work for which, by her natural organization and talent, she is peculiarly adapted.

" Under the first head, our energetic sisters have already, by the help oι their gallant male adjutants, reformed the laws of several of our States, so that a married woman is no longer left the unprotected legal slave of any unprincipled, drunken spendthrift who may be her husband, — but, in case of the imbecility or improvidence of the natural head of the family, the wife, if she have the ability, can conduct business, make contracts, earn and retain money for the good of the household ; and I am sure no one can say that immense injustice and cruelty are not thereby prevented.

" It is quite easy for women who have the good fortune to have just and magnanimous husbands to say that they feel no interest in such reforms, and tha' they would willingly trust their property to the man to whom they give themselves; but they should remember that laws are not made for the restraint of the generous and just, but of the dishonest and base. The law which enables a married woman to hold her own property does not forbid her to give it to the man of her heart, if she so pleases; and it does protect many women who otherwise would be reduced to the extremest misery. I once knew an energetic milliner who had her shop attached four times, and a flourishing business broken up in four different cities, because she was tracked from city to city by a worthless spendthrift, who only waited till she had amassed a little property in a new place to swoop down upon and carry it off. It is to be hoped that the time is not distant when every State will give to woman a fair chance to the ownership and use of her own earnings and her own property.

"Under the head of the right of every woman to do any work for which by natural organization and talent she is especially adapted, there is a word or two to be said.

"The talents and tastes of the majority of women are naturally domestic. The family is evidently their sphere, because in all ways their organization fits them for that more than for anything else.

"But there are occasionally women who are exceptions to the common law, gifted with peculiar genius and adaptations. With regard to such women, there has never seemed to be any doubt in the verdict of mankind, that they ought to follow their nature, and that their particular *sphere* was the one to which they are called. Did anybody ever think that Mrs. Siddons and Mrs. Kemble and Ristori had better have applied themselves sedulously to keeping house, because they were women, and ' woman's noblest station is retreat?'

"The world has always shown a fair average of good sense in this matter, — from the days of the fair Hypatia in Alexandria, who, we are told, gave lectures on philosophy behind a curtain, lest her charms should distract the attention of too impressible young men, down to those of Anna Dickinson. Mankind are not, after all, quite fools, and seem in these cases to have a reasonable idea that exceptional talents have exceptional laws, and make their own code of proprieties.

"Now there is no doubt that Miss Dickinson, though as relating to her femininity she is quite as pretty and modest a young woman as any to be found in the most sheltered circle, has yet a most exceptional talent for public speaking, which draws crowds to hear her, and makes lecturing for her a lucrative profession, as well as a means of advocating just and generous sentiments, and of stimulating her own sex to nobler purposes ; and the same law which relates to Siddons and Kemble and Ristori relates also to her.

" The doctrine of *vocations* is a good one and a safe one. If a woman mistakes her vocation, so much the worse for her ; the world does not suffer, but she does, and the suffering speedily puts her where she belongs. There is not near so much danger from attempts to imitate Anna Dickinson, as there is from the more common feminine attempts to rival the *demi-monde* of Paris in fantastic extravagance and luxury.

" As to how a woman may determine whether she has any such vocation, there is a story quite in point. A good Methodist elder was listening to an ardent young mechanic, who thought he had a call to throw up his shop and go to preaching.

" ' I feel,' said the young ardent, ' that I have a call to preach.'

" ' Hast thou noticed whether people seem to have a call to hear thee ?' said the shrewd old man. ' I have always noticed that a true call of the Lord may be known by this, ' that people have a *call* to hear.' "

" Well," said Bob, " the most interesting question still remains : What are to be the employments of woman ? What ways are there for her to use her talents, to earn her livelihood and support those who are dear to her, when Providence throws that necessity upon her? This is becoming more than ever one of the pressing questions of our age. The war has deprived so many thousands of women of their natural protectors, that everything must be thought of that may possibly open a way for their self-support."

"Well, let us look over the field," said my wife. "What is there for woman?"

"In the first place," said I, "come the professions requiring natural genius, — authorship, painting, sculpture, with the subordinate arts of photographing, coloring, and finishing; but when all is told, these furnish employment to a very limited number, — almost as nothing to the whole. Then there is teaching, which is profitable in its higher branches, and perhaps the very pleasantest of all the callings open to woman; but teaching is at present an overcrowded profession, the applicants everywhere outnumbering the places. Architecture and landscape-gardening are arts every way suited to the genius of woman, and there are enough who have the requisite mechanical skill and mathematical education; and though never yet thought of for the sex, that I know of, I do not despair of seeing those who shall find in this field a profession at once useful and elegant. When women plan dwelling-houses, the vast body of tenements to be let in our cities will wear a more domestic and comfortable air, and will be built more with reference to the real wants of their inmates."

"I have thought," said Bob, "that *agencies* of various sorts, as canvassing the country for the sale of books, maps, and engravings, might properly employ a great many women. There is a large class whose health suffers from confinement and sedentary occupations, who might, I think, be both usefully and agreeably employed in business of this sort, and be recruiting their health at the same time."

"Then," said my wife, "there is the medical profession."

"Yes," said I. "The world is greatly obliged to Miss Blackwell and other noble pioneers who faced and overcame the obstacles to the attainment of a thorough medical education by females. Thanks to them, a new and lucrative profession is now open to educated women in relieving the distresses of their own sex; and we may hope that in time, through their intervention, the care of the sick may also become the vocation of cultivated, refined, intelligent women, instead of being left, as heretofore, to the ignorant and vulgar. The experience of our late war has shown us what women of a high class morally and intellectually can do in this capacity. Why should not this experience inaugurate a new and sacred calling for refined and educated women? Why should not NURSING become a vocation equal in dignity and in general esteem to the medical profession, of which it is the right hand? Why should our dearest hopes, in the hour of their greatest peril, be committed into the hands of Sairey Gamps, when the world has seen Florence Nightingales?"

"Yes, indeed," said my wife; "I can testify, from my own experience, that the sufferings and dangers of the sick-bed, for the want of intelligent, educated nursing, have been dreadful. A prejudiced, pigheaded, snuff-taking old woman, narrow-minded and vulgar, and more confident in her own way than seven men that can render a reason, enters your house at just the hour and moment when all your dearest earthly hopes are brought to a crisis. She becomes absolute dictator over your delicate, helpless wife and your frail babe, — the absolute dictator of all in the house. If it be her sovereign will and pleasure to enact all sorts of physiological absurdities in the premises, who shall say her nay? 'She knows her business, she hopes!' And if it be her edict, as it was of one of her class whom I knew, that each of her babies shall eat four baked beans the day it is four days old, eat them it must; and if the baby die in convulsions four days after, it is set down as the mysterious will of an overruling Providence.

"I know and have seen women lying upon laced pillows under silken curtains, who have been bullied and dominated over in the hour of their greatest helplessness by ignorant and vulgar tyrants, in a way that would scarce be thought possible in civilized society, and children that have been injured or done to death by the same means. A celebrated physician told me of a babe whose eyesight was nearly ruined by its nurse taking a fancy to wash its eyes with camphor, 'to keep it from catching cold,' she said. I knew another infant that was poisoned by the nurse giving it laudanum in some of those patent nostrums which these ignorant creatures carry secretly in their pockets, to secure quiet in their little charges. I knew one delicate woman who never recovered from the effects of being left at her first confinement in the hands of an ill-tempered, drinking nurse, and whose feeble infant was neglected and abused by this woman in a way to cause lasting injury. In the first four weeks of infancy the constitution is peculiarly impressible; and infants of a delicate organization may, if frightened and ill-treated, be the subjects of just such a shock to the nervous system as in mature age comes from the sudden stroke of a great affliction or terror. A bad nurse may affect nerves predisposed to weakness in a manner they never will recover from. I solemnly believe that the constitutions of more women

are broken up by bad nursing in their first confinement than by any other cause whatever. And yet
there are at the same time hundreds and thousands of
women wanting the means of support, whose presence
in a sick-room would be a benediction. I do trust
that Miss Blackwell's band of educated nurses will
not be long in coming, and that the number of such
may increase till they effect a complete revolution in
this vocation. A class of cultivated, well-trained,
intelligent nurses would soon elevate the employment
of attending on the sick into the noble calling it
ought to be, and secure for it its appropriate rewards."

"There is another opening for woman," said I, —
"in the world of business. The system of commer-
cial colleges now spreading over our land is a new
and a most important development of our times.
There that large class of young men who have either
no time or no inclination for an extended classical
education can learn what will fit them for that active
material life which in our broad country needs so
many workers. But the most pleasing feature of these
institutions is, that the complete course is open to
women no less than to men, and women there may
acquire that knowledge of book-keeping and accounts,
and of the forms and principles of business transac-
tions, which will qualify them for some of the lucrative
situations hitherto monopolized by the other sex.

And the expenses of the course of instruction are so arranged as to come within the scope of very moderate means. A fee of fifty dollars entitles a woman to the benefit of the whole course, and she has the privilege of attending at any hours that may suit her own engagements and convenience."

" Then, again," said my wife, " there are the departments of millinery and dressmaking, and the various branches of needle-work, which afford employment to thousands of women ; there is type-setting, by which many are beginning to get a living ; there are the manufactures of cotton, woollen, silk, and the numberless useful articles which employ female hands in their fabrication, — all of them opening avenues by which, with more or less success, a subsistence can be gained."

" Well, really," said Bob, " it would appear, after all, that there are abundance of openings for women. What is the cause of the outcry and distress ? How is it that we hear of women starving, driven to vice and crime by want, when so many doors of useful and profitable employment stand open to them ? "

" The question would easily be solved," said my wife, " if you could once see the kind and class of women who thus suffer and starve. There may be exceptions, but too large a portion of them are girls and women who *can or will do no earthly thing well*, — and what is worse, are not willing to take the pains to be taught to do anything well. I will describe to you one girl, and you will find in every intelligence-office a hundred of her kind to five thoroughly trained ones.

"Imprimis : she is rather delicate and genteel-looking, and you may know from the arrangement of her hair just what the last mode is of disposing of rats or waterfalls. She has a lace bonnet with roses, a silk mantilla, a silk dress trimmed with velvet, a white skirt with sixteen tucks and an embroidered edge, a pair of cloth gaiters, underneath which are a pair of stockings without feet, the only pair in her possession. She has no under-linen, and sleeps at night in the working-clothes she wears in the day. She never seems to have in her outfit either comb, brush, or tooth-brush of her own, — neither needles, thread, scissors, nor pins ; her money, when she has any, being spent on more important articles, such as the lace bonnet or silk mantilla, or the rats and waterfalls that glorify her head. When she wishes to sew, she borrows what is needful of a convenient next neighbor ; and if she gets a place in a family as second girl, she expects to subsist in these respects by borrowing of the better-appointed servants, or helping herself from the family stores.

"She expects, of course, the very highest wages, if she condescends to live out; and by help of a trim outside appearance and the many vacancies that are continually occurring in households, she gets places, where her object is to do just as little of any duty assigned to her as possible, to hurry through her performances, put on her fine clothes, and go a-gadding. She is on free and easy terms with all the men she meets, and ready at jests and repartee, sometimes far from seemly. Her time of service in any one place lasts indifferently from a fortnight to two or three months, when she takes her wages, buys her a new parasol in the latest style, and goes back to the intelligence-office. In the different families where she has lived she has been told a hundred times the proprieties of household life, how to make beds, arrange rooms, wash china, glass, and silver, and set tables ; but her habitual rule is to try in each place how small and how poor services will be accepted. When she finds less will not do, she gives more. When the mistress follows her constantly, and shows an energetic determination to be well served, she shows that she *can* serve well; but the moment such attention relaxes, she slides back again. She is as destructive to a house as a fire ; the very spirit of wastefulness is in her ; she cracks the china, dents the silver, stops the water-pipes with rubbish, and after she is gone, there is generally a sum equal to half her wages to be expended in repairing the effects of her carelessness.

And yet there is one thing to be said for her : she is quite as careful of her employer's things as of her own. The full amount of her mischiefs often does not appear at once, as she is glib of tongue, adroit in apologies, and lies with as much alertness and as little thought of conscience as a blackbird chatters. It is difficult for people who have been trained from child-hood in the school of verities, — who have been lectured for even the shadow of a prevarication, and shut up in disgrace for a lie, till truth becomes a habit of their souls, — it is very difficult for people so edu-cated to understand how to get on with those who never speak the truth except by mere accident, who assert any and everything that comes into their heads with all the assurance and all the energy of perfect verity.

"What becomes of this girl ? She finds means, by begging, borrowing, living out, to keep herself ex-tremely trim and airy for a certain length of time, till the rats and waterfalls, the lace hat and parasol, and the glib tongue, have done their work in making a fool of some honest young mechanic who earns three dollars a day. She marries him with no higher object than to have somebody to earn money for her to spend. And what comes of such marriages ?

"That is *one* ending of her career ; the other is on the street, in haunts of vice, in prison, in drunkenness, and death.

"Whence come these girls? They are as numerous as yellow butterflies in autumn ; they flutter up to
cities from the country ; they grow up from mothers
who ran the same sort of career before them ; and the
reason why in the end they fall out of all reputable
employment and starve on poor wages is, that they
become physically, mentally, and morally incapable of
rendering any service which society will think worth
paying for."

"I remember," said I, "that the head of the most
celebrated dress-making establishment in New York,
in reply to the appeals of the needle-women of the
city for sympathy and wages, came out with published
statements to this effect : that the difficulty lay not in
unwillingness of employers to pay what work was
vorth, but in finding any work worth paying for ; that
she had many applicants, but among them few who
could be of real use to her ; that she, in common with
everybody in this country who has any kind of serious
responsibilities to carry, was continually embarrassed
for want of skilled work-people, who could take and
go on with the labor of her various departments without her constant supervision ; that out of a hundred
girls, there would not be more than five to whom she
could give a dress to be made and dismiss it from her
mind as something certain to be properly done.

"Let people individually look around their own lit-

tle sphere, and ask themselves if they know any woman really excelling in any *valuable* calling or accomplishment who is suffering for want of work. All of
us know seamstresses, dress-makers, nurses, and laun-
dresses, who have made themselves such a reputation,
and are so beset and overcrowded with work, that the
whole neighborhood is constantly on its knees to them
with uplifted hands. The fine seamstress, who can
cut and make trousseaus and layettes in elegant perfection, is always engaged six months in advance ; the
pet dress-maker of a neighborhood must be engaged
in May for September, and in September for May ; a
laundress who sends your clothes home in nice order
always has all the work that she can do. Good work
in any department is the rarest possible thing in our
American life ; and it is a fact that the great majority
of workers, both in the family and out, do only toler-
ably well, — not so badly that it actually cannot be
borne, yet not so well as to be a source of real,
thorough satisfaction. The exceptional worker in
every neighborhood, who does things really *well*, can
always set her own price, and is always having more
offering than she can possibly do.

"The trouble, then, in finding employment for women lies deeper than the purses or consciences of the
employers ; it lies in the want of education in women ,
the want of *education*, I say, — meaning by education

that which fits a woman for practical and profitable employment in life, and not mere common school learning."

"Yes," said my wife ; "for it is a fact that the most troublesome and hopeless persons to provide for are often those who have a good medium education, but no feminine habits, no industry, no practical calculation, no muscular strength, and no knowledge of any one of woman's peculiar duties. In the earlier days of New England, women, as a class, had far fewer opportunities for acquiring learning, yet were far better educated, physically and morally, than now. The high school did not exist ; at the common school they learned reading, writing, and arithmetic, and practised spelling ; while at home they did the work of the household. They were cheerful, bright, active, ever on the alert, able to do anything, from the harnessing and driving of a horse to the finest embroidery. The daughters of New England in those days looked the world in the face without a fear. They shunned no labor ; they were afraid of none ; and they could always find their way to a living."

"But although less instructed in school learning," said I, "they showed no deficiency in intellectual acumen. I see no such women, nowadays, as some I remember of that olden time, — women whose strong minds and ever active industry carried on

3   D

reading and study side by side with household toils.

"I remember a young lady friend of mine, attending a celebrated boarding-school, boarded in the family of a woman who had never been to school longer than was necessary to learn to read and write, yet who was a perfect cyclopedia of general information. The young scholar used to take her Chemistry and Natural Philosophy into the kitchen, where her friend was busy with her household work, and read her lessons to her, that she might have the benefit of her explanations ; and so, while the good lady scoured her andirons or kneaded her bread, she lectured to her *protégée* on mysteries of science far beyond the limits of the text-book. Many of the graduates of our modern high schools would find it hard to shine in conversation on the subjects they had studied, in the searching presence of some of these vigorous matrons of the olden time, whose only school had been the leisure hours gained by energy and method from their family cares."

"And in those days," said my wife, "there lived in our families a class of American domestics, women of good sense and good powers of reflection, who applied this sense and power of reflection to household matters. In the early part of my married life, I myself had American 'help' ; and they were not only excel lent servants, but trusty and invaluable friends. But now, all this class of applicants for domestic service have disappeared, I scarce know why or how. All I know is, there is no more a Betsey or a Lois, such as used to take domestic cares off my shoulders so completely."

"Good heavens! where are they?" cried Bob. "Where do they hide? I would search through the world after such a prodigy!"

"The fact is," said I, "there has been a slow and gradual reaction against household labor in America. Mothers began to feel that it was a sort of *curse*, to be spared, if possible, to their daughters; women began to feel that they were fortunate in proportion as they were able to be entirely clear of family responsibilities. Then Irish labor began to come in, simultaneously with a great advance in female education.

"For a long while nothing was talked of, written of, thought of, in teachers' meetings, conventions, and assemblies, but the neglected state of female education; and the whole circle of the arts and sciences was suddenly introduced into our free-school system, from which needle-work as gradually and quietly was suffered to drop out. The girl who attended the primary and high school had so much study imposed on her that she had no time for sewing or housework; and the delighted mother was only too happy to darn her stockings and do the house-work alone, that her daughter might rise to a higher plane than she herself had attained to. The daughter, thus educated, had, on coming to womanhood, no solidity of muscle, no manual dexterity, no practice or experience in domestic life; and if she were to seek a livelihood, there remained only teaching, or some feminine trade, or the factory."

"These factories," said my wife, "have been the ruin of hundreds and hundreds of our once healthy farmers' daughters and others from the country. They go there young and unprotected; they live there in great boarding-houses, and associate with a pro-miscuous crowd, without even such restraints of mater-nal supervision as they would have in great boarding-schools; their bodies are enfeebled by labor often necessarily carried on in a foul and heated atmos-phere; and at the hours when off duty, they are ex-posed to all the dangers of unwatched intimacy with the other sex.

"Moreover, the factory-girl learns and practises but one thing, — some one mechanical movement, which gives no scope for invention, ingenuity, or any other of the powers called into play by domestic labor; so that she is in reality unfitted in every way for family duties.

"Many times it has been my lot to try, in my fam

fty service, girls who have left factories ; and I have
found them wholly useless for any of the things which
a woman ought to be good for. They knew nothing
of a house, or what ought to be done in it ; they had
imbibed a thorough contempt of household labor, and
looked upon it but as a *dernier ressort;* and it was only
the very lightest of its tasks that they could even begin to think of. I remember I tried to persuade one
of these girls, the pretty daughter of a fisherman, to
take some lessons in washing and ironing. She was
at that time engaged to be married to a young mechanic, who earned something like two or three dollars
a day.

" ' My child,' said I, 'you will need to understand
all kinds of housework, if you are going to be married.'

" She tossed her little head, —

" ' Indeed, she was n't going to trouble herself about
that.'

" ' But who will get up your husband's shirts ? '

" ' O, he must put them out. I 'm not going to be
married to make a slave of myself ! '

" Another young factory-girl, who came for table
and parlor work, was so full of airs and fine notions,
that it seemed as difficult to treat with her as with a
princess. She could not sweep, because it blistered
her hands, which, in fact, were long and delicate ; she

could not think of putting them into hot dish-water, and for that reason preferred washing the dishes in cold water ; she required a full hour in the morning to make her toilet ; she was laced so tightly that she could not stoop without vertigo, and her hoops were of dimensions which seemed to render it impossible for her to wait upon table ; she was quite exhausted with the effort of ironing the table-napkins and chamber-towels ; — yet she could not think of 'living out' under two dollars a week.

"Both these girls had had a good free-school education, and could read any amount of novels, write a tolerable letter, but had not learned anything with sufficient accuracy to fit them for teachers. They were pretty, and their destiny was to marry and lie a dead weight on the hands of some honest man, and to increase, in their children, the number of incapables."

"Well," said Bob, "what would you have? What is to be done?"

"In the first place," said I, "I would have it felt by those who are seeking to elevate woman, that the work is to be done, not so much by creating for her new spheres of action as by elevating her conceptions of that domestic vocation to which God and Nature have assigned her. It is all very well to open to her avenues of profit and advancement in the great outer world ; but, after all, *to make and keep a home* is, and ever must be, a woman's first glory, her highest aim. No work of art can compare with a perfect home ; the training and guiding of a family must be recognized as the highest work a woman can perform ; and female education ought to be conducted with special reference to this.

" Men are *trained* to be lawyers, to be physicians, to be mechanics, by long and self-denying study and practice. A man cannot even make shoes merely by going to the high school, and learning reading, writing, and mathematics ; he cannot be a book-keeper or a printer simply from general education.

" Now women have a sphere and profession of their own, — a profession for which they are fitted by physical organization, by their own instincts, and to which they are directed by the pointing and manifest finger of God, — and that sphere is *family life.*

" Duties to the State and to public life they may have ; but the public duties of women must bear to their family ones the same relation that the family duties of men bear to their public ones.

" The defect in the late efforts to push on female education is, that it has been for her merely general, and that it has left out and excluded all that is professional ; and she undertakes the essential duties of womanhood, when they do devolve on her, without any adequate preparation."

"But is it possible for a girl to learn at school the things which fit her for family life ?" said Bob.

"Why not?" I replied. "Once it was thought impossible in schools to teach girls geometry, or algebra, or the higher mathematics ; it was thought impossible to put them through collegiate courses; but it has been done, and we see it. Women study treatises on political economy in schools ; and why should not the study of domestic economy form a part of every school course ? A young girl will stand up at the blackboard, and draw and explain the compound blowpipe, and describe all the process of making oxygen and hydrogen. Why should she not draw and explain a refrigerator as well as an air-pump ? Both are to be explained on philosophical principles. When a school-girl, in her Chemistry, studies the reciprocal action of acids and alkalies, what is there to hinder the teaching her its application to the various processes of cooking where acids and alkalies are employed ? Why should she not be led to see how effervescence and fermentation can be made to perform their office in the preparation of light and digestible bread ? Why should she not be taught the chemical substances by which food is often adulterated, and the tests by which such adulterations are detected ? Why should she not understand the processes of confectionery, and know how to guard against the deleterious or poisonous elements that are introduced into children's sugar-plums and candies? Why, when she learns the doctrine of *mordants*, the substances by which different colors are set, should she not learn it with some practical view to future life, so that she may know how to set the color of a fading calico or restore the color of a spotted one? Why, in short, when a girl has labored through a profound chemical work, and listened to courses of chemical lectures, should she come to domestic life, which presents a constant series of chemical experiments and changes, and go blindly along as without chart or compass, unable to tell what will take out a stain, or what will brighten a metal, what are common poisons and what their antidotes, and not knowing enough of the laws of caloric to understand how to warm a house, or of the laws of atmosphere to know how to ventilate one? Why should the preparation of food, that subtile art on which life, health, cheerfulness, good temper, and good looks so largely depend, for-ever be left in the hands of the illiterate and vulgar?

"A benevolent gentleman has lately left a large fortune for the founding of a university for women; and the object is stated to be to give women who have already acquired a general education the means of acquiring a professional one, to fit themselves for some employment by which they may gain a livelihood.

3*

" In this institution the women are to be instructed in book-keeping, stenography, telegraphing, photographing, drawing, modelling, and various other arts ; but so far as I remember, there is no proposal to teach domestic economy as at least *one* of woman's professions.

" Why should there not be a professor of domestic economy in every large female school ? Why should not this professor give lectures, first on house-planning and building, illustrated by appropriate apparatus ? Why should not the pupils have presented to their inspection models of houses planned with reference to economy, to ease of domestic service, to warmth, to ventilation, and to architectural appearance ? Why should not the professor go on to lecture further on house-fixtures, with models of the best mangles, washing-machines, clothes-wringers, ranges, furnaces, and cooking-stoves, together with drawings and apparatus illustrative of domestic hydraulics, showing the best contrivances for bathing-rooms and the obvious principles of plumbing, so that the pupils may have some idea how to work the machinery of a convenient house when they have it, and to have such conveniences introduced when wanting? If it is thought worth while to provide, at great expense, apparatus for teaching the revolutions of Saturn's moons and the precession of the equinoxes, why should there not be some also to teach what it may greatly concern a woman's earthly happiness to know?

"Why should not the professor lecture on home-chemistry, devoting his first lecture to bread-making? and why might not a batch of bread be made and baked and exhibited to the class, together with specimens of morbid anatomy in the bread line, — the sour cotton bread of the baker, — the rough, big-holed bread, — the heavy, fossil bread, — the bitter bread of too much yeast, — and the causes of their defects pointed out? And so with regard to the various articles of food, — why might not chemical lectures be given on all of them, one after another? In short, it would be easy to trace out a course of lectures on common things to occupy a whole year, and for which the pupils, whenever they come to have homes of their own, will thank the lecturer to the last day of their life.

"Then there is no impossibility in teaching needle-work, the cutting and fitting of dresses, in female schools. The thing is done very perfectly in English schools for the working classes. A girl trained at one of these schools came into a family I once knew. She brought with her a sewing-book, in which the process of making various articles was exhibited in miniature. The several parts of a shirt were first shown, each perfectly made, and fastened to a leaf of the book by itself, and then the successive steps of uniting the parts, till finally appeared a miniature model of the whole. The sewing was done with red thread, so that every stitch might show, and any imperfection be at once remedied. The same process was pursued with regard to other garments, and a good general idea of cutting and fitting them was thus given to an entire class of girls.

"In the same manner the care and nursing of young children and the tending of the sick might be made the subject of lectures. Every woman ought to have some general principles to guide her with regard to what is to be done in case of the various accidents that may befall either children or grown people, and of their lesser illnesses, and ought to know how to pre-pare comforts and nourishment for the sick. Haw-thorne's satirical remarks upon the contrast between the elegant Zenobia's conversation and the smoky porridge she made for him when he was an invalid might apply to the volunteer cookery of many charm-ing women."

"I think," said Bob, "that your Professor of Do-mestic Economy would find enough to occupy his pupils."

"In fact," said I, "were domestic economy properly honored and properly taught, in the manner described it would open a sphere of employment to so many women in the home life, that we should not be obliged to send our women out to California or the Pacific to put an end to an anxious and aimless life.

"When domestic work is sufficiently honored to be taught as an art and science in our boarding-schools and high schools, then possibly it may acquire also dignity in the eyes of our working classes, and young girls who have to earn their own living may no longer feel degraded in engaging in domestic service. The place of a domestic in a family may become as respectable in their eyes as a place in a factory, in a printing-office, in a dressmaking or millinery establishment, or behind the counter of a shop.

"In America there is no class which will confess itself the lower class, and a thing recommended solely for the benefit of any such class finds no one to receive it.

"If the intelligent and cultivated look down on household work with disdain ; if they consider it as degrading, a thing to be shunned by every possible device ; they may depend upon it that the influence of such contempt of woman's noble duties will flow downward, producing a like contempt in every class in life.

"Our sovereign princesses learn the doctrine of equality very quickly, and are not going to sacrifice themselves to what is not considered *de bon ton* by the upper classes; and the girl with the laced hat and parasol, without under-clothes, who does her best to 'shirk' her duties as housemaid, and is looking for marriage as an escape from work, is a fair copy of her mistress, who married for much the same reason, who hates housekeeping, and would rather board or do anything else than have the care of a family; — the one is about as respectable as the other.

"When housekeeping becomes an enthusiasm, and its study and practice a fashion, then we shall have in America that class of persons to rely on for help in household labors who are now going to factories, to printing-offices, to every kind of toil, forgetful of the best life and sphere of woman."

III.

A FAMILY–TALK ON RECONSTRUCTION.

OUR Chimney-Corner, of which we have spoken somewhat, has, besides the wonted domestic circle, its *habitués* who have a frequent seat there. Among these, none is more welcome than Theophilus Thoro.

Friend Theophilus was born on the shady side of Nature, and endowed by his patron saint with every grace and gift which can make a human creature worthy and available, except the gift of seeing the bright side of things. His bead-roll of Christian virtues includes all the graces of the spirit except hope ; and so, if one wants to know exactly the flaw, the defect, the doubtful side, and to take into account all the untoward possibilities of any person, place, or thing, he had best apply to friend Theophilus. He can tell you just where and how the best-laid scheme is likely to fail. just the screw that will fall loose in the smoothest-working machinery, just the flaw in the most perfect character, just the defect in the best-written book, just the variety of thorn that must accompany each particular species of rose.

Yet Theophilus is without guile or malice. His want of faith in human nature is not bitter and censorious, but melting and pitiful. "We are all poor trash, miserable dogs together," he seems to say, as he looks out on the world and its ways. There is not much to be expected of or for any of us ; but let us love one another, and be patient.

Accordingly, Theophilus is one of the most incessant workers for human good, and perseveringly busy in every scheme of benevolent enterprise, in all which he labors with melancholy steadiness without hope. In religion he has the soul of a martyr, — nothing would suit him better than to be burned alive for his faith ; but his belief in the success of Christianity is about on a par with that of the melancholy disciple of old, who, when Christ would go to Judæa, could only say, " Let us also go, that we may die with him." Theophilus is always ready to die for the truth and the right, for which he never sees anything but defeat and destruction ahead.

During the late war, Theophilus has been a despairing patriot, dying daily, and giving all up for lost in every reverse from Bull Run to Fredericksburg. The surrender of Richmond and the capitulation of Lee shortened his visage somewhat; but the murder of the President soon brought it back to its old length. It is true, that, while Lincoln lived, he was in a perpetual state of dissent from all his measures. He had broken his heart for years over the miseries of the slaves, but he shuddered at the Emancipation Proclamation; a whirlwind of anarchy was about to sweep over the country, in which the black and the white would dash against each other, and be shivered like potters' vessels. He was in despair at the accession of Johnson, — believing the worst of the unfavorable reports that clouded his reputation. Nevertheless, he was among the first of loyal citizens to rally to the support of the new administration, because, though he had no hope in that, he could see nothing better.

You must not infer from all this that friend Theophilus is a social wet blanket, a goblin shadow at the domestic hearth. By no means. Nature has gifted him with that vein of humor and that impulse to friendly joviality which are frequent developments in sad-natured men, and often deceive superficial observers as to their real character. He who laughs well and makes you laugh is often called a man of cheerful disposition; yet in many cases nothing can be further from it than precisely this kind of person.

Theophilus frequents our chimney-corner, perhaps

E

because Mrs. Crowfield and myself are, so to speak, children of the light and the day. My wife has precisely the opposite talent to that of our friend. She can discover the good point, the sound spot, where others see only defect and corruption. I myself am somewhat sanguine, and prone rather to expect good than evil, and with a vast stock of faith in the excellent things that may turn up in the future. The Millennium is one of the prime articles of my creed ; and all the ups and downs of society I regard only as so many jolts on a very rough road that is taking the world on, through many upsets and disasters, to that final consummation.

Theophilus holds the same belief, theoretically ; but it is apt to sink so far out of sight in the mire of present disaster as to be of very little comfort to him.

"Yes," he said, "we are going to ruin, in my view, about as fast as we can go. Miss Jennie, I will trouble you for another small lump of sugar in my tea."

"You have been saying that, about our going to ruin, every time you have taken tea here for four years past," said Jennie ; "but I always noticed that your fears never spoiled your relish either for tea or muffins. People talk about being on the brink of a volcano and the country going to destruction, and all that just as they put pepper on their potatoes; it is an agreeable stimulant in conversation, — that's all."

"For my part," said my wife, "I can speak in another vein. When had we ever in all our history so *bright* prospects, so much to be thankful for? Slavery is abolished; the last stain of disgrace is wiped from our national honor. We stand now before the world self-consistent with our principles. We have come out of one of the severest struggles that ever tried a nation, purer and stronger in morals and religion, as well as more prosperous in material things."

"My dear madam, excuse me," said Theophilus; "but I cannot help being reminded of what an English reviewer once said, — that a lady's facts have as much poetry in them as Tom Moore's lyrics. Of course poetry is always agreeable, even though of no statistical value."

"I see no poetry in my facts," said Mrs. Crowfield. "Is not slavery forever abolished, by the confession of its best friends, — even of those who declare its abolition a misfortune, and themselves ruined in consequence?"

"I confess, my dear madam, that we have succeeded as we human creatures commonly do, in supposing that we have destroyed an evil, when we have only changed its name. We have contrived to withdraw from the slave just that fiction of property relation which made it for the interest of some one to care for him a little, however imperfectly; and having destroyed that, we turn him out defenceless to shift for himself in a community every member of which is imbittered against him. The whole South resounds with the outcries of slaves suffering the vindictive wrath of former masters; laws are being passed hunting them out of this State and out of that; the animosity of race — at all times the most bitter and unreasonable of animosities — is being aroused all over the land. And the Free States take the lead in injustice to them. Witness a late vote of Connecticut on the suffrage question. The efforts of government to protect the rights of these poor defenceless creatures are about as energetic as such efforts always have been and always will be while human nature remains what it is. For a while the obvious rights of the weaker party will be confessed, with some show of consideration, in public speeches; they will be paraded by philanthropic sentimentalists, to give point to their eloquence; they will be here and there sustained in governmental measures, when there is no strong temptation to the contrary, and nothing better to be done; but the moment that political combinations begin to be formed, all the rights and interests of this helpless people will be bandied about as so many make-weights in the political scale. Any troublesome lion will have a negro thrown to him to keep him quiet. All their hopes will be dashed to the ground by the imperious Southern white, no longer feeling for them even the interest of a master, and regarding them with a mixture of hatred and loathing as the cause of all his reverses. Then if, driven to despair, they seek to defend themselves by force, they will be crushed by the power of the government, and ground to powder, as the weak have always been under the heel of the strong.

" So much for our abolition of slavery. As to our material prosperity, it consists of an inflated paper currency, an immense debt, a giddy, foolhardy spirit of speculation and stock-gambling, and a perfect furor of extravagance, which is driving everybody to live beyond his means, and casting contempt on the republican virtues of simplicity and economy.

" As to advancement in morals, there never was so much intemperance in our people before, and the papers are full of accounts of frauds, defalcations, forgeries, robberies, assassinations, and arsons. Against this tide of corruption the various organized denominations of religion do nothing effectual. They are an army shut up within their own intrenchments, holding their own with difficulty, and in no situation to turn back the furious assaults of the enemy."

" In short," said Jennie " according to your showing, the whole country is going to destruction. Now, if things really are so bad, if you really believe all you have been saying, you ought not to be sitting drinking your tea as you are now, or to have spent the afternoon playing croquet with us girls ; you ought to gird yourself with sackcloth, and go up and down the land, raising the alarm, and saying, ' Yet forty days and Nineveh shall be overthrown.' "

"Well," said Theophilus, while a covert smile played about his lips, " you know the saying, ' Let us eat and drink, for to-morrow,' etc. Things are not yet *gone* to destruction, only *going*, — and why not have a good time on deck before the ship goes to pieces ? Your chimney-corner is a tranquil island in the ocean of trouble, and your muffins are absolutely perfect. I 'll take another, if you 'll please to pass them."

" I 've a great mind *not* to pass them," said Jennie. " Are you in earnest in what you are saying ? or are you only saying it for sensation ? How *can* people believe such things and be comfortable ? *I* could not. If I believed all you have been saying I could not sleep nights, — I should be perfectly miserable ; and *you* cannot really believe all this, or you would be."

" My dear child," said Mrs. Crowfield, " our friend's picture is the truth painted with all its shadows and none of its lights. All the dangers he speaks of are **real** and great, but he omits the counterbalancing good. Let *me* speak now. There never has been a time in our history when so many honest and just men held power in our land as now, — never a government before in which the public councils recognized with more respect the just and the right. There never was an instance of a powerful government showing more tenderness in the protection of a weak and defenceless race than ours has shown in the care of the freedmen hitherto. There never was a case in which the people of a country were more willing to give money and time and disinterested labor to raise and educate those who have thus been thrown on their care. Considering that we have had a great, harassing, and expensive war on our hands, I think the amount done by government and individuals for the freedmen unequalled in the history of nations; and I do not know why it should be predicted from this past fact, that, in the future, both government and people are about to throw them to the lions, as Mr. Theophilus supposes. Let us wait, at least, and see. So long as government maintains a freedmen's bureau, administered by men of such high moral character, we must think, at all events, that there are strong indications in the right direction. Just think of the immense advance of public opinion within four years, and of the grand successive steps of this advance, — Emancipation in the District of Columbia, the Repeal of the

Fugitive Slave Law, the General Emancipation **Act,** the Amendment of the Constitution. All these do not look as if the black were about to be ground to powder beneath the heel of the white. If the negroes are oppressed in the South, they can emigrate; no laws hold them; active, industrious laborers will soon find openings in any part of the Union."

"No," said Theophilus, "there will be black laws like those of Illinois and Tennessee, there will be turbulent uprisings of the Irish, excited by political demagogues, that will bar them out of Northern States. Besides, as a class, they *will* be idle and worthless. It will not be their fault, but it will be the result of their slave education. All their past observation of their masters has taught them that liberty means licensed laziness, that work means degradation, — and therefore they will loathe work, and cherish laziness as the sign of liberty. 'Am not I free? Have I not as good a right to do nothing as you?' will be the cry.

"Already the lazy whites, who never lifted a hand in any useful employment, begin to raise the cry that 'niggers won't work'; and I suspect the cry may not be without reason. Industrious citizens can never be made in a community where the higher class think useful labor a disgrace. The whites will oppose the negro in every effort to rise; they will debar him of every civil and social right; they will set him the worst possible example, as they have been doing for hundreds of years; and then they will hound and hiss at him for being what they made him. This is the old track of the world, — the good, broad, reputable road on which all aristocracies and privileged classes have been always travelling; and it's not likely that we shall have much of a secession from it. The Millennium is n't so near us as that, by a great deal."

"It's all very well arguing from human selfishness and human sin in that way," said I; "but you can't take up a newspaper that does n't contain abundant facts to the contrary. Here, now," — and I turned to the Tribune, — "is one item that fell under my eye accidentally, as you were speaking: —

"'The Superintendent of Freedmen's Affairs in Louisiana, in making up his last Annual Report, says he has 1,952 blacks settled temporarily on 9,650 acres of land, who last year raised crops to the value of $175,000, and that he had but few worthless blacks under his care; and that, as a class, the blacks have fewer vagrants than can be found among any other class of persons.'

"Such testimonies gem the newspapers like stars."

"Newspapers of your way of thinking, very likely," said Theophilus; "but if it comes to statistics, I can bring counter-statements, numerous and dire, from

4

scores of Southern papers, of vagrancy, laziness, improvidence, and wretchedness."

"Probably both are true," said I, "according to the greater or less care which has been taken of the blacks in different regions. Left to themselves, they tend downward, pressed down by the whole weight of semi-barbarous white society ; but when the free North protects and guides, the results are as you see."

"And do you think the free North has salt enough in it to save this whole Southern mass from corruption ? I wish I could think so ; but all I can see in the free North at present is a raging, tearing, headlong chase after *money*. Now money is of significance only as it gives people the power of expressing their ideal of life. And what does this ideal prove to be among us ? Is it not to ape all the splendors and vices of old aristocratic society ? Is it not to be able to live in idleness, without useful employment, a life of glitter and flutter and show ? What do our New York dames of fashion seek after ? To avoid family care, to find servants at any price who will relieve them of home responsibilities, and take charge of their houses and children while they shine at ball and opera, and drive in the park. And the servants who learn of these mistresses, — what do they seek after ? *They* seek also to get rid of care, to live as nearly as possible without work, to dress and shine in their secondary sphere, as the mistresses do in the primary one. High wages with little work and plenty of company express Biddy's ideal of life, which is a little more respectable than that of her mistress, who wants high wages with no work. The house and the children are not Biddy's ; and why should she care more for their well-being than the mistress and the mother?

"Hence come wranglings and moanings. Biddy uses a chest of tea in three months, and the amount of the butcher's bill is fabulous ; Jane gives the baby laudanum to quiet it, while she slips out to *her* parties ; and the upper classes are shocked at the demoralized state of the Irish, their utter want of faithfulness and moral principle ! How dreadful that there are no people who enjoy the self-denials and the cares which they dislike, that there are no people who rejoice in carrying that burden of duties which they do not wish to touch with one of their fingers ! The outcry about the badness of servants means just this : that everybody is tired of self-helpfulness, — the servants as thoroughly as the masters and mistresses. All want the cream of life, without even the trouble of skimming ; and the great fight now is, who shall drink the skim-milk, which nobody wants. *Work,* — honorable toil, — manly, womanly endeavor, — is just what nobody likes ; and this is as much a fact in the free North as in the slave South.

"What are all the young girls looking for in marriage? Some man with money enough to save them from taking any care or having any trouble in domestic life, enabling them, like the lilies of the field, to rival Solomon in all his glory, while they toil not, neither do they spin ; and when they find that even money cannot purchase freedom from care in family life, because their servants are exactly of the same mind with themselves, and hate to do their duties as cordially as they themselves do, then are they in anguish of spirit, and wish for slavery, or aristocracy, or anything that would give them power over the lower classes."

"But surely, Mr. Theophilus," said Jennie, " there is no sin in disliking trouble, and wanting to live easily and have a good time in one's life, — it 's so very natural."

"No sin, my dear, I admit ; but there is a certain amount of work and trouble that somebody must take to carry on the family and the world ; and the mischief is, that all are agreed in wanting to get rid of it. Human nature is above all things lazy. I am lazy myself. Everybody is. The whole struggle of society is as to who shall eat the hard bread-and-cheese of labor, which must be eaten by somebody. Nobody wants it, — neither you in the parlor, nor Biddy in the kitchen.

" ' The mass ought to labor, and *we* lie on sofas,' is

a sentence that would unite more subscribers than any confession of faith that ever was presented, whether religious or political; and its subscribers would be as numerous and sincere in the Free States as in the Slave States, or I am much mistaken in my judgment. The negroes are men and women, like any of the rest of us, and particularly apt in the imitation of the ways and ideas current in good society; and consequently to learn to play on the piano, and to have nothing in particular to do, will be the goal of aspiration among colored girls and women, and to do housework will seem to them intolerable drudgery, simply because it is so among the fair models to whom they look up in humble admiration. You see, my dear, what it is to live in a democracy. It deprives us of the vantage-ground on which we cultivated people can stand and say to our neighbor, — 'The cream is for me, and the skim-milk for you; the white bread for me, and the brown for you. I am born to amuse myself and have a good time, and you are born to do everything that is tiresome and disagreeable to me.' The 'My Lady Ludlows' of the Old World can stand on their platform and lecture the lower classes from the Church Catechism, to 'order themselves lowly and reverently to all their betters'; and they can base their exhortations on the old established law of society by which some are born to inherit the earth, and live a life of ease and pleasure, and others to toil without pleasure or amusement, for their support and aggrandizement.   An aristocracy as I take it, is a combination of human beings to divide life into two parts, one of which shall comprise all social and moral advantages, refinement, elegance, leisure, ease, pleasure, and amusement, — and the other, incessant toil, with the absence of every privilege and blessing of human existence.   Life thus divided, we aristocrats keep the good for ourselves and our children, and distribute the evil as the lot of the general mass of mankind.   The desire to monopolize and to dominate is the most rooted form of human selfishness ; it is the hydra with many heads, and, cut off in one place, it puts out in another.

"Nominally, the great aristocratic arrangement of American society has just been destroyed ; but really, I take it, the essential *animus* of the slave system still exists, and pervades the community, North as well as South.   Everybody is wanting to get the work done by somebody else, and to take the money himself ; the grinding between employers and employed is going on all the time, and the field of controversy has only been made wider by bringing in a whole new class of laborers.   The Irish have now the opportunity to sustain their aristocracy over the negro.   Shall they not have somebody to look down upon ?

" All through free society, employers and employed are at incessant feud; and the more free and enlightened the society, the more bitter the feud. The standing complaint of life in America is the badness of servants; and England, which always follows at a certain rate behind us in our social movements, is beginning to raise very loudly the same complaint. The condition of service has been thought worthy of public attention in some of the leading British prints; and Ruskin, in a summing-up article, speaks of it as a deep ulcer in society, — a thing hopeless of remedy."

" My dear Mr. Theophilus," said my wife, " I cannot imagine whither you are rambling, or to what purpose you are getting up these horrible shadows. You talk of the world as if there were no God in it, overruling the selfishness of men, and educating it up to order and justice. I do not deny that there is a vast deal of truth in what you say. Nobody doubts that, in general, human nature *is* selfish, callous, unfeeling, willing to engross all good to itself, and to trample on the rights of others. Nevertheless, thanks to God's teaching and fatherly care, the world has worked along to the point of a great nation founded on the principles of strict equality, forbidding all monopolies, aristocracies, privileged classes, by its very constitution; and now, by God's wonderful providence, this nation has been brought, and forced, as it were, to overturn and abolish the only aristocratic institution that interfered with its free development. Does not this look as if a Mightier Power than ours were working in and for us, supplementing our weakness and infirmity? and if we believe that man is always ready to drop everything and let it run back to evil, shall we not have faith that God will *not* drop the noble work he has so evidently taken in hand in this nation?"

"And I want to know," said Jennie, "why your illustrations of selfishness are all drawn from the female sex. Why do you speak of *girls* that marry for money, any more than men? of *mistresses* of families that want to be free from household duties and responsibilities, rather than of masters?"

"My charming young lady," said Theophilus, "it is a fact that in America, except the slaveholders, women have hitherto been the only aristocracy. Women have been the privileged class, — the only one to which our rough democracy has always and everywhere given the precedence, — and consequently the vices of aristocrats are more developed in them as a class than among men. The leading principle of aristocracy, which is to take pay without work, to live on the toils and earnings of others, is one which obtains more generally among women than among men in this country. The men of our country, as a general thing, even in our uppermost classes, always propose to themselves some work or business by which they may acquire a fortune, or enlarge that already made for them by their fathers. The women of the same class propose to themselves nothing but to live at their ease on the money made for them by the labors of fathers and husbands. As a consequence, they become enervated and indolent, — averse to any bracing, wholesome effort, either mental or physical. The unavoidable responsibilities and cares of a family, instead of being viewed by them in the light of a noble life-work, in which they do their part in the general labors of the world, seem to them so many injuries and wrongs ; they seek to turn them upon servants, and find servants unwilling to take them ; and so selfish are they, that I have heard more than one lady declare that she did n't care if it was unjust, she should like to have slaves, rather than be plagued with servants who had so much liberty. All the novels, poetry, and light literature of the world, which form the general staple of female reading, are based upon aristocratic institutions, and impregnated with aristocratic ideas ; and women among us are constantly aspiring to foreign and aristocratic modes of life rather than to those of native, republican simplicity. How many women are there, think you, that would

4 *   F

not go in for aristocracy and aristocratic prerogatives, if they were only sure that they themselves should be of the privileged class? To be ' My Lady Duchess,' and to have a right by that simple title to the prostrate deference of all the lower orders! How many would have firmness to vote against such an establishment merely because it was bad for society? Tell the fair Mrs. Feathercap, 'In order that you may be a duchess, and have everything a paradise of elegance and luxury around you and your children, a hundred poor families must have no chance for anything better than black bread and muddy water all their lives, a hundred poor men must work all their lives on such wages that a fortnight's sickness will send their families to the almshouse, and that no amount of honesty and forethought can lay up any provision for old age.' "

" Come now, sir," said Jennie, " don't tell me that there are any girls or women so mean and selfish as to want aristocracy or rank so purchased! You are too bad, Mr. Theophilus! "

" Perhaps they might not, were it stated in just these terms; yet I think, if the question of the establishment of an order of aristocracy among us were put to vote, we should find more women than men who would go for it; and they would flout at the consequences to society with the lively wit and the musical laugh which make feminine selfishness so genteel and agreeable

"No! It is a fact, that, in America, the women, in the wealthy classes, are like the noblemen of aristocracies, and the men are the workers. And in all this outcry that has been raised about women's wages being inferior to those of men there is one thing overlooked, — and that is, that women's work is generally inferior to that of men, because in every rank they are the pets of society, and are excused from the laborious drill and training by which men are fitted for their callings. Our fair friends come in generally by some royal road to knowledge, which saves them the dire necessity of real work, — a sort of feminine hop-skip-and-jump into science or mechanical skill, — nothing like the uncompromising hard labor to which the boy is put who would be a mechanic or farmer, a lawyer or physician.

"I admit freely that we men are to blame for most of the faults of our fair nobility. There is plenty of heroism, abundance of energy, and love of noble endeavor lying dormant in these sheltered and petted daughters of the better classes ; but *we* keep it down and smother it. Fathers and brothers think it discreditable to themselves not to give their daughters and sisters the means of living in idleness ; and any adventurous fair one, who seeks to end the ennui of utter aimlessness by applying herself to some occupation whereby she may earn her own living, infallibly

draws down on her the comments of her whole circle :
—'Keeping school, is she? Is n't her father rich
enough to support her? What could possess her?'"

"I am glad, my dear Sir Oracle, that you are
beginning to recollect yourself and temper your severi-
ties on our sex," said my wife. "As usual, there is
much truth lying about loosely in the vicinity of your
assertions ; but they are as far from being in themselves the truth as would be their exact opposites.

"The class of American women who travel, live
abroad, and represent our country to the foreign eye,
have acquired the reputation of being Sybarites in
luxury and extravagance, and there is much in the
modes of life that are creeping into our richer circles
to justify this.

"Miss Murray, ex-maid-of-honor to the Queen of
England, among other impressions which she received
from an extended tour through our country, states it
as her conviction that young American girls of the
better classes are less helpful in nursing the sick and
in the general duties of family life than the daughters
of the aristocracy of England ; and I am inclined to
believe it, because even the Queen has taken special
pains to cultivate habits of energy and self-helpfulness
in her children. One of the toys of the Princess
Royal was said to be a cottage of her own, furnished
with every accommodation for cooking and house-

keeping, where she from time to time enacted the part of housekeeper, making bread and biscuit, boiling potatoes which she herself had gathered from her own garden-patch, and inviting her royal parents to meals of her own preparing ; and report says, that the dignitaries of the German court have been horrified at the energetic determination of the young royal housekeeper to overlook her own linen-closets and attend to her own affairs. But as an offset to what I have been saying, it must be admitted that America is a country where a young woman can be self-supporting without forfeiting her place in society. All our New England and Western towns show us female teachers who are as well received and as much caressed in society, and as often contract advantageous marriages, as any women whatever ; and the productive labor of American women, in various arts, trades, and callings, would be found, I think, not inferior to that of any women in the world.

" Furthermore, the history of the late war has shown them capable of every form of heroic endeavor. We have had hundreds of Florence Nightingales, and an amount of real hard work has been done by female hands not inferior to that performed by men in the camp and field, and enough to make sure that American womanhood is not yet so enervated as seriously to interfere with the prospects of free republican society."

" I wonder," said Jennie, " what it is in our country that spoils the working-classes that come into it. They say that the emigrants, as they land here, are often simple-hearted people, willing to work, accustomed to early hours and plain living, decorous and respectful in their manners. It would seem as if aristocratic drilling had done them good. In a few months they become brawling, impertinent, grasping, want high wages, and are very unwilling to work. I went to several intelligence-offices the other day to look for a girl for Marianne, and I thought, by the way the candidates catechized the ladies, and the airs they took upon them, that they considered themselves the future mistresses interrogating their subordinates.

" ' Does ye expect me to do the washin' with the cookin' ? '

" ' Yes.'

" ' Thin I 'll niver go to that place ! '

" ' And does ye expect me to get the early breakfast for yer husband to be off in the train every mornin' ? '

" ' Yes.'

" ' I niver does that, — that ought to be a second girl's work.'

" ' How many servants does ye keep, ma'am ? '

" ' Two.'

" ' I niver lives with people that keeps but two servants.'

" ' How many has ye in yer family ?'

" ' Seven.'

" ' That 's too large a family. Has ye much company ?'

" ' Yes, we have company occasionally.'

" ' Thin I can't come to ye; it 'll be too harrd a place.'

" In fact, the thing they were all in quest of seemed to be a very small family, with very high wages, and many perquisites and privileges.

" This is the kind of work-people our manners and institutions make of people that come over here. I remember one day seeing a coachman touch his cap to his mistress when she spoke to him, as is the way in Europe, and hearing one or two others saying among themselves, —

" ' That chap 's a greenie; he 'll get over that soon.' "

" All these things show," said I, " that the staff of power has passed from the hands of gentility into those of labor. We may think the working-classes somewhat unseemly in their assertion of self-importance; but, after all, are they, considering their inferior advantages of breeding, any more overbearing and impertinent than the upper classes have always been to them in all ages and countries ?

" When Biddy looks long, hedges in her work with

many conditions, and is careful to get the most she can for the least labor, is she, after all, doing any more than you or I or all the rest of the world? I myself will not write articles for five dollars a page, when there are those who will give me fifteen. I would not do double duty as an editor on a salary of seven thousand, when I could get ten thousand for less work.

"Biddy and her mistress are two human beings, with the same human wants. Both want to escape trouble, to make their life comfortable and easy, with the least outlay of expense. Biddy's capital is her muscles and sinews ; and she wants to get as many greenbacks in exchange for them as her wit and shrewdness will enable her to do. You feel, when you bargain with her, that she is nothing to you, except so far as her strength and knowledge may save you care and trouble ; and she feels that you are nothing to her, except so far as she can get your money for her work. The free-and-easy airs of those seeking employment show one thing, — that the country in general is prosperous, and that openings for profitable employment are so numerous that it is not thought necessary to try to conciliate favor. If the community were at starvation-point, and the loss of a situation brought fear of the almshouse, the laboring-class would be more subservient. As it is, there is a little spice of the bitterness of a past age of servitude in their present attitude, — a bristling, self-defensive impertinence, which will gradually smooth away as society learns to accommodate itself to the new order of things."

"Well, but, papa," said Jennie, " don't you think all this a very severe test, if applied to us women particularly, more than to the men? Mr. Theophilus seems to think women are aristocrats, and go for enslaving the lower classes out of mere selfishness; but I say that we are a great deal more strongly tempted than men, because all these annoyances and trials of domestic life come upon us. It is very insidious, the aristocratic argument, as it appeals to us ; there seems much to be said in its favor. It does appear to me that it is better to have servants and work-people tidy, industrious, respectful, and decorous, as they are in Europe, than domineering, impertinent, and negligent, as they are here, — and it seems that there is something in our institutions that produces these disagreeable traits ; and I presume that the negroes will eventually be travelling the same road as the Irish, and from the same influences.

"When people see all these things, and feel all the inconveniences of them, I don't wonder that they are tempted not to like democracy, and to feel as if aristocratic institutions made a more agreeable state of society. It is not such a blank, bald, downright piece of brutal selfishness as Mr. Theophilus there seems to suppose, for us to wish there were some quiet, submissive, laborious lower class, who would be content to work for kind treatment and moderate wages."

"But, my little dear," said I, "the matter is not left to our choice. Wish it or not wish it, it's what we evidently can't have. The day for that thing is past. The power is passing out of the hands of the culti-vated few into those of the strong, laborious many. *Numbers* is the king of our era ; and he will reign over us, whether we will hear or whether we will for-bear. The sighers for an obedient lower class and the mourners for slavery may get ready their crape, and have their pocket-handkerchiefs bordered with black ; for they have much weeping to do, and for many years to come. The good old feudal times, when two thirds of the population thought themselves born only for the honor, glory, and profit of the other third, are gone, with all their beautiful devotions, all their trappings of song and story. In the land where such institutions were most deeply rooted and most firmly established, they are assailed every day by hard hands and stout hearts ; and their position resembles that of some of the picturesque ruins of Italy, which are constantly being torn away to build prosaic mod ern shops and houses.

" This great democratic movement is coming down into modern society with a march as irresistible as the glacier moves down from the mountains. Its front is in America, — and behind are England, France, Italy, Prussia, and the Mohammedan countries. In all, the rights of the laboring masses are a living force, bearing slowly and inevitably all before it. Our war has been a marshalling of its armies, commanded by a hard-handed, inspired man of the working-class. An intelligent American, recently resident in Egypt, says it was affecting to notice the interest with which the working-classes there were looking upon our late struggle in America, and the earnestness of their wishes for the triumph of the Union. 'It is our cause, it is for us,' they said, as said the cotton-spinners of England and the silk-weavers of Lyons. The forces of this mighty movement are still directed by a man from the lower orders, the sworn foe of exclusive privileges and landed aristocracies. If Andy Johnson is consistent with himself, with the principles which raised him from a tailor's bench to the head of a mighty nation, he will see to it that the work that Lincoln began is so thoroughly done, that every man and every woman in America, of whatever race or complexion, shall have exactly equal rights before the law, and be free to rise or fall according to their individual intelligence, industry, and moral worth. So long as everything is not strictly in accordance with our principles of democracy, so long as there is in any part of the country an aristocratic upper class who despise labor, and a laboring lower class that is denied equal political rights, so long this grinding and discord between the two will never cease in America. It will make trouble not only in the South, but in the North, — trouble between all employers and employed, — trouble in every branch and department of labor, — trouble in every parlor and every kitchen.

"What is it that has driven every American woman out of domestic service, when domestic service is full as well paid, is easier, healthier, and in many cases far more agreeable, than shop and factory work? It is, more than anything else, the influence of slavery in the South, — its insensible influence on the minds of mistresses, giving them false ideas of what ought to be the position and treatment of a female citizen in domestic service, and its very marked influence on the minds of freedom-loving Americans, causing them to choose *any* position rather than one which is regarded as assimilating them to slaves. It is difficult to say what are the very worst results of a system so altogether bad as that of slavery; but one of the worst is certainly the utter contempt it brings on useful labor, and the consequent utter physical and moral degradation of a large body of the whites; and this contempt of useful labor has been constantly spreading like an infection from the Southern to the Northern States, particularly among women, who, as our friend here has truly said, are by our worship and exaltation of them made peculiarly liable to take the malaria of aristocratic society. Let anybody observe the conversation in good society for an hour or two, and hear the tone in which servant-girls, seamstresses, mechanics, and all who work for their living, are sometimes mentioned, and he will see, that, while every one of the speakers professes to regard useful labor as respectable, she is yet deeply imbued with the leaven of aristocratic ideas.

"In the South the contempt for labor bred of slavery has so permeated society, that we see great, coarse, vulgar *lazzaroni* lying about in rags and vermin, and dependent on government rations, maintaining, as their only source of self-respect, that they never have done and never *will* do a stroke of useful work, in all their lives. In the North there are, I believe, no *men* who would make such a boast; but I think there are many women — beautiful, fascinating *lazzaroni* of the parlor and boudoir — who make their boast of elegant helplessness and utter incompetence for any of woman's duties with equal *naïveté*. The Spartans made their slaves drunk, to teach their children the evils of intoxication; and it seems to be the policy of a large class in the South now to keep down and degrade the only working-class they have, for the sake of teaching their children to despise work.

"We of the North, who know the dignity of labor who know the value of free and equal institutions, who have enjoyed advantages for seeing their operation, ought, in true brotherliness, to exercise the power given us by the present position of the people of the Southern States, and put things thoroughly right *for* them, well knowing, that, though they may not like it at the moment, they will like it in the end, and that it will bring them peace, plenty, and settled prosperity, such as they have long envied here in the North. It is no kindness to an invalid brother, half recovered from delirium, to leave him a knife to cut his throat with, should he be so disposed. We should rather appeal from Philip drunk to Philip sober, and do real kindness, trusting to the future for our meed of gratitude.

"Giving equal political rights to all the inhabitants of the Southern States will be their shortest way to quiet and to wealth. It will avert what is else almost certain, — a war of races ; since all experience shows that the ballot introduces the very politest relations between the higher and lower classes. If the right be restricted, let it be by requirements of property and education, applying to all the population equally.

"Meanwhile, we citizens and citizenesses of the North should remember that Reconstruction means something more than setting things right in the Southern States. We have saved our government and institutions, but we have paid a fearful price for their salvation ; and we ought to prove now that they are worth the price.

"The empty chair, never to be filled, — the light gone out on its candlestick, never on earth to be rekindled, —gallant souls that have exhaled to heaven in slow torture and starvation, — the precious blood that has drenched a hundred battle-fields, — all call to us with warning voices, and tell us not to let such sacrifices be in vain. They call on us by our clear understanding of the great principles of democratic equality, for which our martyred brethren suffered and died, to show to all the world that their death was no mean and useless waste, but a glorious investment for the future of mankind.

"This war, these sufferings, these sacrifices, ought to make every American man and woman look on himself and herself as belonging to a royal priesthood, a peculiar people. The blood of our slain ought to be a gulf, wide and deep as the Atlantic, dividing us from the opinions and the practices of countries whose government and society are founded on other and antagonistic ideas. Democratic republicanism has never yet been perfectly worked out either in this or any other country. It is a splendid edifice, half built, deformed by rude scaffolding, noisy with the clink of trowels, blinding the eyes with the dust of lime, and endangering our heads with falling brick. We make our way over heaps of shavings and lumber to view the stately apartments, — we endanger our necks in climbing ladders standing in the place of future staircases; but let us not for all this cry out that the old rat-holed mansions of former ages, with their mould, and moss, and cockroaches, are better than this new palace. There is no lime-dust, no clink of trowels, no rough scaffolding there, to be sure, and life goes on very quietly; but there is the foul air of slow and sure decay.

"Republican institutions in America are in a transition state; they have not yet separated themselves from foreign and antagonistic ideas and traditions, derived from old countries; and the labors necessary for the upbuilding of society are not yet so adjusted that there is mutual pleasure and comfort in the relations of employer and employed. We still incline to class-distinctions and aristocracies. We incline to the scheme of dividing the world's work into two orders: first, physical labor, which is held to be rude and vulgar, and the province of a lower class; and second, brain labor, held to be refined and aristocratic, and the province of a higher class. Meanwhile, the Creator, who is the greatest of levellers, has given to every human being *both* a physical system, needing to be kept in order by physical labor, and an intellectual or brain power, needing to be kept in order by brain labor. *Work*, use, employment, is the condition of health in both ; and he who works either to the neglect of the other lives but a half-life, and is an imperfect human being.

" The aristocracies of the Old World claim that their only labor should be that of the brain ; and they keep their physical system in order by violent exercise, which is made genteel from the fact only that it is not useful or productive. It would be losing caste to refresh the muscles by handling the plough or the axe ; and so foxes and hares must be kept to be hunted, and whole counties turned into preserves, in order that the nobility and gentry may have physical exercise in a way befitting their station, — that is to say, in a way that produces nothing, and does good only to themselves.

" The model republican uses his brain for the highest purposes of brain work, and his muscles in *productive* physical labor ; and useful labor he respects above that which is merely agreeable.

" When this equal respect for physical and mental labor shall have taken possession of every American

5   G

citizen, there will be no so-called laboring class; there will no more be a class all muscle without brain power to guide it, and a class all brain without muscular power to execute. The labors of society will be lighter, because each individual will take his part in them ; they will be performed better, because no one will be overburdened.

"In those days, Miss Jennie, it will be an easier matter to keep house, because, housework being no longer regarded as degrading drudgery, you will find a superior class of women ready to engage in it.

"Every young girl and woman, who in her sphere and by her example shows that she is not ashamed of domestic labor, and that she considers the necessary work and duties of family life as dignified and important, is helping to bring on this good day. Louis Philippe once jestingly remarked, — 'I have this qualification for being a king in these days, that I have blacked my own boots, and could black them again.'

"Every American ought to cultivate, as his pride and birthright, the habit of self-helpfulness. Our command of the labors of good *employés* in any department is liable to such interruptions, that he who has blacked his own boots, and can do it again, is, on the whole, likely to secure the most comfort in life.

"As to that which Mr. Ruskin pronounces to be a

deep, irremediable ulcer in society, namely, domestic service, we hold that the last workings of pure democracy will cleanse and heal it. When right ideas are sufficiently spread, — when everybody is self-helpful and capable of being self-supporting, — when there is a fair start for every human being in the race of life, and all its prizes are, without respect of persons, to be obtained by the best runner, — when every kind of useful labor is thoroughly respected, — then there will be a clear, just, wholesome basis of intercourse on which employers and employed can move without wrangling or discord.

" Renouncing all claims to superiority on the one hand, and all thought of servility on the other, service can be rendered by fair contracts and agreements, with that mutual respect and benevolence which every human being owes to every other.

" But for this transition period, which is wearing out the life of so many women, and making so many households uncomfortable, I have some alleviating suggestions, which I shall give in my next chapter."

IV.

IS WOMAN A WORKER?

"PAPA, do you see what the Evening Post says of your New-Year's article on Reconstruction?" said Jennie, as we were all sitting in the library after tea.

"I have not seen it."

"Well, then, the charming writer, whoever he is, takes up for us girls and women, and maintains that no work of any sort ought to be expected of us; that our only mission in life is to be beautiful, and to refresh and elevate the spirits of men by being so. If I get a husband, my mission is to be always becomingly dressed, to display most captivating toilettes, and to be always in good spirits, — as, under the circumstances, I always should be, — and thus 'renew his spirits' when he comes in weary with the toils of life. Household cares are to be far from me: they destroy my cheerfulness and injure my beauty.

"He says that the New England standard of excellence as applied to woman has been a mistaken one; and, in consequence, though the girls are beautiful, the matrons are faded, overworked, and uninteresting; and that such a state of society tends to immorality, because, when wives are no longer charming, men are open to the temptation to desert their firesides, and get into mischief generally. He seems particularly to complain of your calling ladies who do nothing the 'fascinating *lazzaroni* of the parlor and boudoir.'"

"There was too much truth back of that arrow not to wound," said Theophilus Thoro, who was ensconced, as usual, in his dark corner, whence he supervises our discussions.

"Come, Mr. Thoro, we won't have any of your bitter moralities," said Jennie; "they are only to be taken as the invariable bay-leaf which Professor Blot introduces into all his recipes for soups and stews, — a little elegant bitterness, to be kept tastefully in the background. You see now, papa, I should like the vocation of being beautiful. It would just suit me to wear point-lace and jewelry, and to have life revolve round me, as some beautiful star, and feel that I had nothing to do but shine and refresh the spirits of all gazers, and that in this way I was truly useful, and fulfilling the great end of my being; but alas for this doctrine! all women **have** not beauty. The most of us can only hope not to be called ill-looking, and, when we get ourselves up with care, to look fresh and trim and agreeable; which fact interferes with the theory."

"Well, for my part," said young Rudolph, "I go for the theory of the beautiful. If ever I marry, it is to find an asylum for ideality. I don't want to make a culinary marriage or a business partnership. I want a being whom I can keep in a sphere of poetry and beauty, out of the dust and grime of every-day life."

"Then," said Mr. Theophilus, "you must either be a rich man in your own right, or your fair ideal must have a handsome fortune of her own."

"I never will marry a rich wife," quoth Rudolph. "My wife must be supported by me, not I by her."

Rudolph is another of the *habitués* of our chimney-corner, representing the order of young knight-hood in America, and his dreams and fancies, if impracticable, are always of a kind to make every one think him a good fellow. He who has no romantic dreams at twenty-one will be a horribly dry peascod at fifty; therefore it is that I gaze reverently at all Rudolph's chateaus in Spain, which want nothing to complete them except solid earth to stand on.

"And pray," said Theophilus, "how long will it take a young lawyer or physician, starting with no heritage but his own brain, to create a sphere of poetry and beauty in which to keep his goddess? How much a year will be necessary, as the English say, to *do* this garden of Eden, whereinto shall enter only the poetry of life?"

"I don't know. I have n't seen it near enough to consider. It is because I know the difficulty of its attainment that I have no present thoughts of marriage. Marriage is to me in the bluest of all blue distances, — far off, mysterious, and dreamy as the Mountains of the Moon or sources of the Nile. It shall come only when I have secured a fortune that shall place my wife above all necessity of work or care."

"I desire to hear from you," said Theophilus, "when you have found the sum that will keep a woman from care. I know of women now inhabiting palaces, waited on at every turn by servants, with carriages, horses, jewels, laces, cashmeres, enough for princesses, who are eaten up by care. One lies awake all night on account of a wrinkle in the waist of her dress; another is dying because no silk of a certain inexpressible shade is to be found in New York; a third has had a dress sent home, which has proved such a failure that life seems no longer worth having. If it were not for the consolations of religion, one does n't know what would become of her. The fact is, that care and labor are as much correlated to human existence as shadow is to light; there is no such thing as excluding them from any mortal lot. You may make a canary-bird or a goldfish live in absolute contentment without a care or labor, but a human being you cannot. Human beings are restless and active in their very nature, and will do something, and that something will prove a care, a labor, and a fatigue, arrange it how you will. As long as there is anything to be desired and not yet attained, so long its attainment will be attempted; so long as that attainment is doubtful or difficult, so long will there be care and anxiety. When boundless wealth releases woman from every family care, she immediately makes herself a new set of cares in another direction, and has just as many anxieties as the most toilful housekeeper, only they are of a different kind. Talk of labor, and look at the upper classes in London or in New York in the fashionable season. Do any women work harder? To rush from crowd to crowd all night, night after night, seeing what they are tired of, making the agreeable over an abyss of inward yawning, crowded, jostled, breathing hot air, and crushed in halls and stairways, without a moment of leisure for months and months, till

brain and nerve and sense reel, and the country is
longed for as a period of resuscitation and relief!
Such is the release from labor and fatigue brought
by wealth. The only thing that makes all this labor
at all endurable is, that it is utterly and entirely useless, and does no good to any one in creation ; this
alone makes it genteel, and distinguishes it from the
vulgar toils of a housekeeper. These delicate creatures, who can go to three or four parties a night
for three months, would be utterly desolate if they
had to watch one night in a sick-room ; and though
they can exhibit any amount of physical endurance
and vigor in crowding into assembly rooms, and
breathe tainted air in an opera-house with the most
martyr-like constancy, they could not sit one half-
hour in the close room where the sister of charity
spends hours in consoling the sick or aged poor."

" Mr. Theophilus is quite at home now," said Jennie ; " only start him on the track of fashionable life,
and he takes the course like a hound. But hear,
now, our champion of the Evening Post : —

"'The instinct of women to seek a life of repose,
their eagerness to attain the life of elegance, does not
mean contempt for labor, but it is a confession of
unfitness for labor. Women were not intended to
work, — not because work is ignoble, but because it
is as disastrous to the beauty of a woman as is fric-

5*

tion to the bloom and softness of a flower. Woman is to be kept in the garden of life; she is to rest, to receive, to praise; she is to be kept from the workshop world, where innocence is snatched with rude hands, and softness is blistered into unsightliness or hardened into adamant. No social truth is more in need of exposition and illustration than this one; and, above all, the people of New England need to know it, and, better, they need to believe it.

"'It is therefore with regret that we discover Christopher Crowfield applying so harshly, and, as we think so indiscriminatingly, the theory of work to women, and teaching a society made up of women sacrificed in the workshops of the state, or to the dust-pans and kitchens of the house, that women must work, ought to work, and are dishonored if they do not work; and that a woman committed to the drudgery of a household is more creditably employed than when she is charming, fascinating, irresistible, in the parlor or boudoir. The consequence of this fatal mistake is manifest throughout New England, — in New England, where the girls are all beautiful and the wives and mothers faded, disfigured, and without charm or attractiveness. The moment a girl marries in New England she is apt to become a drudge, or a lay figure on which to exhibit the latest fashions. She never has beautiful hands, and she would not have a beauti

ful face if a utilitarian society could " apply " her face
to anything but the pleasure of the eye. Her hands
lose their shape and softness after childhood, and
domestic drudgery destroys her beauty of form and
softness and bloom of complexion after marriage. To
correct, or rather to break up, this despotism of
household cares, or of work, over woman, American
society must be taught that women will inevitably fade
and deteriorate, unless it insures repose and comfort
to them. It must be taught that reverence for beauty
is the normal condition, while the theory of work,
applied to women, is disastrous alike to beauty and
morals. Work, when it is destructive to men or women, is forced and unjust.

" ' All the great masculine or creative epochs have
been distinguished by spontaneous work on the part
of men, and universal reverence and care for beauty.
The praise of work, and sacrifice of women to this
great heartless devil of work, belong only to, and are
the social doctrine of, a mechanical age and a utilitarian epoch. And if the New England idea of social
life continues to bear so cruelly on woman, we shall
have a reaction somewhat unexpected and shocking.' "

"Well now, say what you will," said Rudolph, " you
have expressed my idea of the conditions of the sex.
Woman was not made to work ; she was made to be
taken care of by man. All that is severe and trying,

whether in study or in practical life, is and ought to
be in its very nature essentially the work of the male
sex. The value of woman is precisely the value of
those priceless works of art for which we build mu-
seums, — which we shelter and guard as the world's
choicest heritage ; and a lovely, cultivated, refined
woman, thus sheltered, and guarded, and developed,
has a worth that cannot be estimated by any gross,
material standard. So I subscribe to the sentiments
of Miss Jennie's friend without scruple."

"The great trouble in settling all these society questions," said I, "lies in the gold-washing, — the cra-
dling I think the miners call it. If all the quartz were
in one stratum and all the gold in another, it would
save us a vast deal of trouble. In the ideas of Jennie's friend of the Evening Post there is a line of
truth and a line of falsehood so interwoven and
threaded together that it is impossible wholly to assent or dissent. So with your ideas, Rudolph, there
is a degree of truth in them, but there is also a fal-
lacy.

"It is a truth, that woman as a sex ought not to do
the hard work of the world, either social, intellectual,
or moral. There are evidences in her physiology that
this was not intended for her, and our friend of the
Evening Post is right in saying that any country will
advance more rapidly in civilization and refinement

where woman is thus sheltered and protected. And I think, furthermore, that there is no country in the world where women *are* so much considered and cared for and sheltered, in every walk of life, as in America. In England and France, — all over the continent of Europe, in fact, — the other sex are deferential to women only from some presumption of their social standing, or from the fact of acquaintanceship ; but among strangers, and under circumstances where no particular rank or position can be inferred, a woman travelling in England or France is jostled and pushed to the wall, and left to take her own chance, precisely as if she were not a woman. Deference to delicacy and weakness, the instinct of protection, does not appear to characterize the masculine population of any other quarter of the world so much as that of America. In France, *les Messieurs* will form a circle round the fire in the receiving-room of a railroad station, and sit, tranquilly smoking their cigars, while ladies who do not happen to be of their acquaintance are standing shivering at the other side of the room. In England, if a lady is incautiously booked for an outside place on a coach, in hope of seeing the scenery, and the day turns out hopelessly rainy, no gentleman in the coach below ever thinks of offering to change seats with her, though it pour torrents. In America, the roughest backwoods steamboat or canal-boat captain always, as a matter of course, considers himself charged with the protection of the ladies. ' *Place aux dames* ' is written in the heart of many a shaggy fellow who could not utter a French word any more than could a buffalo. It is just as I have before said, — women are the recognized aristocracy, the *only* aristocracy, of America ; and, so far from regarding this fact as objectionable, it is an unceasing source of pride in my country.

"That kind of knightly feeling towards woman which reverences her delicacy, her frailty, which protects and cares for her, is, I think, the crown of manhood ; and without it a man is only a rough animal. But our fair aristocrats and their knightly defenders need to be cautioned lest they lose their position, as many privileged orders have before done, by an arrogant and selfish use of power.

"I have said that the vices of aristocracy are more developed among women in America than among men, and that, while there are no men in the Northern States who are not ashamed of living a merely idle life of pleasure, there are many women who make a boast of helplessness and ignorance in woman's family duties which any man would be ashamed to make with regard to man's duties, as if such helplessness and ignorance were a grace and a charm.

"There are women who contentedly live on, year

after year, a life of idleness, while the husband and
father is straining every nerve, growing prematurely
old and gray, abridged of almost every form of recreation or pleasure, — all that he may keep them in a
state of careless ease and festivity. It may be very
fine, very generous, very knightly, in the man who
thus toils at the oar that his princesses may enjoy
their painted voyages ; but what is it for the women?

"A woman is a moral being — an immortal soul
— before she is a woman ; and as such she is charged
by her Maker with some share of the great burden of
work which lies on the world.

"Self-denial, the bearing of the cross, are stated by
Christ as indispensable conditions to the entrance into
his kingdom, and no exception is made for man or
woman. Some task, some burden, some cross, each
one must carry; and there must be something done
in every true and worthy life, not as amusement, but
as duty, — not as play, but as earnest *work*, — and no
human being can attain to the Christian standard
without this.

"When Jesus Christ took a towel and girded himself, poured water into a basin, and washed his disciples' feet, he performed a significant and sacrament
al act, which no man or woman should ever forget.
If wealth and rank and power absolve from the services of life, then certainly were Jesus Christ absolved,

as he says, — 'Ye call me Master, and Lord. If I, then, your Lord and Master, have washed your feet, ye also ought to wash one another's feet. For I have given you an example, that ye should do as I have done to you.'

"Let a man who seeks to make a terrestrial paradise for the woman of his heart, — to absolve her from all care, from all labor, — to teach her to accept and to receive the labor of others without any attempt to offer labor in return, — consider whether he is not thus going directly against the fundamental idea of Christianity, — taking the direct way to make his idol selfish and exacting, to rob her of the highest and noblest beauty of womanhood.

"In that chapter of the Bible where the relation between man and woman is stated, it is thus said, with quaint simplicity : 'It is not good that the man should be alone ; I will make him an *help meet* for him.' Woman the *helper* of man, not his toy, — not a picture, not a statue, not a work of art, but a HELPER, a doer, — such is the view of the Bible and the Christian religion.

"It is not necessary that women should work physically or morally to an extent which impairs beauty. In France, where woman is harnessed with an ass to the plough which her husband drives, — where she digs, and wields the pickaxe, — she becomes prematurely hideous ; but in America, where woman reigns as queen in every household, she may surely be a good and thoughtful housekeeper, she may have physical strength exercised in lighter domestic toils, not only without injuring her beauty, but with manifest advantage to it. Almost every growing young girl would be the better in health, and therefore handsomer, for two hours of active housework daily ; and the habit of usefulness thereby gained would be an equal advantage to her moral development. The labors of modern, well-arranged houses are not in any sense severe ; they are as gentle as any kind of exercise that can be devised, and they bring into play muscles that ought to be exercised to be healthily developed.

"The great danger to the beauty of American women does not lie, as the writer of the Post contends, in an overworking of the physical system which shall stunt and deform ; on the contrary, American women of the comfortable classes are in danger of a loss of physical beauty from the entire deterioration of the muscular system for want of exercise. Take the life of any American girl in one of our large towns, and see what it is. We have an educational system of public schools which for intellectual culture is a just matter of pride to any country. From the time that the girl is seven years old, her first thought, when

H

she rises in the morning, is to eat her breakfast and be off to her school. There really is no more time than enough to allow her to make that complete toilet which every well-bred female ought to make, and to take her morning meal before her school begins. She returns at noon with just time to eat her dinner, and the afternoon session begins. She comes home at night with books, slate, and lessons enough to occupy her evening. What time is there for teaching her any household work, for teaching her to cut or fit or sew, or to inspire her with any taste for domestic duties? Her arms have no exercise; her chest and lungs, and all the complex system of muscles which are to be perfected by quick and active movement, are compressed while she bends over book and slate and drawing-board; while the ever-active brain is kept all the while going at the top of its speed. She grows up spare, thin, and delicate; and while the Irish girl, who sweeps the parlors, rubs the silver, and irons the muslins, is developing a finely rounded arm and bust, the American girl has a pair of bones at her sides, and a bust composed of cotton padding, the work of a skilful dress-maker. Nature, who is no respecter of persons, gives to Colleen Bawn, who uses her arms and chest, a beauty which perishes in the gentle, languid Edith, who does nothing but study and read."

"But is it not a fact," said Rudolph, "as stated by

our friend of the Post, that American matrons are perishing, and their beauty and grace all withered, from overwork?"

"It is," said my wife; "but why? It is because they are brought up without vigor or muscular strength, without the least practical experience of household labor, or those means of saving it which come by daily practice; and then, after marriage, when physically weakened by maternity, embarrassed by the care of young children, they are often suddenly deserted by every efficient servant, and the whole machinery of a complicated household left in their weak, inexperienced hands. In the country, you see a household perhaps made void some fine morning by Biddy's sudden departure, and nobody to make the bread, or cook the steak, or sweep the parlors, or do one of the complicated offices of a family, and no bakery, cook-shop, or laundry to turn to for alleviation. A lovely, refined home becomes in a few hours a howling desolation; and then ensues a long season of breakage, waste, distraction, as one wild Irish immigrant after another introduces the style of Irish cottage life into an elegant dwelling.

"Now suppose I grant to the Evening Post that woman ought to rest, to be kept in the garden of life, and all that, how is this to be done in a country where a state of things like this is the commonest of occur-

rences? And is it any kindness or reverence to woman, to educate her for such an inevitable destiny by
a life of complete physical delicacy and incapacity?
Many a woman who has been brought into these cruel
circumstances would willingly exchange all her knowledge of German and Italian, and all her graceful accomplishments, for a good physical development, and
some respectable *savoir faire* in ordinary life.

"Moreover, American matrons are overworked because some unaccountable glamour leads them to continue to bring up their girls in the same inefficient
physical habits which resulted in so much misery to
themselves. Housework as they are obliged to do it,
untrained, untaught, exhausted, and in company with
rude, dirty, unkempt foreigners, seems to them a degradation which they will spare to their daughters.
The daughter goes on with her schools and accomplishments, and leads in the family the life of an elegant little visitor during all those years when a young
girl might be gradually developing and strengthening
her muscles in healthy household work. It never
occurs to her that she can or ought to fill any of the
domestic gaps into which her mother always steps,
and she comforts herself with the thought, 'I don't
know how; I can't; I have n't the strength. I *can'*
sweep; it blisters my hands. If I should stand at
the ironing-table an hour, I should be ill for a week.

As to cooking, I don't know anything about it.' And so, when the cook, or the chambermaid, or nurse, or all together, vacate the premises, it is the mamma who is successively cook, and chambermaid, and nurse; and this is the reason why matrons fade and are over worked.

"Now, Mr. Rudolph, do you think a woman any less beautiful or interesting because she is a fully developed physical being, — because her muscles have been rounded and matured into strength, so that she can meet the inevitable emergencies of life without feeling them to be distressing hardships? If there be a competent, well-trained servant to sweep and dust the parlor, and keep all the machinery of the house in motion, she may very properly select her work out of the family, in some form of benevolent helpfulness; but when the inevitable evil hour comes, which is likely to come first or last in every American household, is a woman any less an elegant woman because her love of neatness, order, and beauty leads her to make vigorous personal exertions to keep her own home undefiled? For my part, I think a disorderly, ill-kept home, a sordid, uninviting table, has driven more husbands from domestic life than the unattractiveness of any overworked woman. So long as a woman makes her home harmonious and orderly, so long as the hour of assembling around the family table is something to be looked forward to as a comfort and a refreshment, a man cannot see that the good house fairy, who by some magic keeps everything so delightfully, has either a wrinkle or a gray hair.

"Besides," said I, "I must tell you, Rudolph, what you fellows of twenty-one are slow to believe; and that is, that the kind of ideal paradise you propose in marriage, is, in the very nature of things, an impossibility, — that the familiarities of every-day life between two people who keep house together must and will destroy it. Suppose you are married to Cytherea herself, and the next week attacked with a rheumatic fever. If the tie between you is that of true and honest love, Cytherea will put on a gingham wrapper, and with her own sculptured hands wring out the flannels which shall relieve your pains; and she will be no true woman if she do not prefer to do this to employing any nurse that could be hired. True love ennobles and dignifies the material labors of life; and homely services rendered for love's sake have in them a poetry that is immortal.

"No true-hearted woman can find herself, in real, actual life, unskilled and unfit to minister to the wants and sorrows of those dearest to her, without a secret sense of degradation. The feeling of uselessness is an extremely unpleasant one. Tom Hood, in a very humorous paper, describes a most accomplished schoolmistress, a teacher of all the arts and crafts which are supposed to make up fine gentlewomen, who is stranded in a rude German inn, with her father writhing in the anguish of a severe attack of gastric inflammation. The helpless lady gazes on her suffering parent, longing to help him, and thinking over all her various little store of accomplishments, not one of which bear the remotest relation to the case. She could knit him a bead-purse, or make him a guard-chain, or work him a footstool, or festoon him with cut tissue-paper, or sketch his likeness, or crust him over with alum crystals, or stick him over with little rosettes of red and white wafers ; but none of these being applicable to his present case, she sits gazing in resigned imbecility, till finally she desperately resolves to improvise him some gruel, and, after a laborious turn in the kitchen, — after burning her dress and blacking her fingers, — succeeds only in bringing him a bowl of *paste!*

"Not unlike this might be the feeling of many an elegant and accomplished woman, whose education has taught and practised her in everything that woman ought to know, except those identical ones which fit her for the care of a home, for the comfort of a sick-room ; and so I say again, that, whatever a woman may be in the way of beauty and elegance, she must have the strength and skill of a *practical worker*, or she is nothing. She is not simply to *be* the beautiful, — she is to *make* the beautiful, and preserve it ; and she who makes and she who keeps the beautiful must be able *to work*, and know how to work. Whatever offices of life are performed by women of culture and refinement are thenceforth elevated ; they cease to be mere servile toils, and become expressions of the ideas of superior beings. If a true lady makes even a plate of toast, in arranging a *petit souper* for her invalid friend, she does it as a lady should. She does not cut blundering and uneven slices ; she does not burn the edges ; she does not deluge it with bad butter, and serve it cold ; but she arranges and serves all with an artistic care, with a nicety and delicacy, which make it worth one's while to have a lady friend in sickness.

"And I am glad to hear that Monsieur Blot is teaching classes of New York ladies that cooking is not a vulgar kitchen toil, to be left to blundering servants, but an elegant feminine accomplishment, better worth a woman's learning than crochet or embroidery ; and that a well-kept culinary apartment may be so inviting and orderly that no lady need feel her ladyhood compromised by participating in its pleasant toils. I am glad to know that his cooking academy is thronged with more scholars than he can accommodate, and from ladies in the best classes of society.

"Moreover, I am glad to see that in New Bedford, recently, a public course of instruction in the art of bread-making has been commenced by a lady, and that classes of the most respectable young and married ladies in the place are attending them.

"These are steps in the right direction, and show that our fair countrywomen, with the grand good-sense which is their leading characteristic, are resolved to supply whatever in our national life is wanting.

"I do not fear that women of such sense and energy will listen to the sophistries which would persuade them that elegant imbecility and inefficiency are charms of cultivated womanhood or ingredients in the poetry of life. She alone can keep the poetry and beauty of married life who has this poetry in her soul ; who with energy and discretion can throw back and out of sight the sordid and disagreeable details which beset all human living, and can keep in the foreground that which is agreeable ; who has enough knowledge of practical household matters to make unskilled and rude hands minister to her cultivated and refined tastes, and constitute her skilled brain the guide of unskilled hands. From such a home, with such a mistress, no sirens will seduce a man,

6

even though the hair grow gray, and the merely physical charms of early days gradually pass away. The enchantment that was about her person alone in the days of courtship seems in the course of years to have interfused and penetrated the *home* which she has created, and which in every detail is only an expression of her personality.   Her thoughts, her plans, her provident care, are everywhere; and the *home* attracts and holds by a thousand ties the heart which before marriage was held by the woman alone."

V.

THE TRANSITION.

"THE fact is, my dear," said my wife, "that you have thrown a stone into a congregation of blackbirds, in writing as you have of our family wars and wants. The response comes from all parts of the country, and the task of looking over and answering your letters becomes increasingly formidable. Everybody has something to say, — something to propose."

"Give me a *résumé*," said I.

"Well," said my wife, "here are three pages from an elderly gentleman, to the effect that women are not what they used to be, — that daughters are a great care and no help, — that girls have no health and no energy in practical life, — that the expense of maintaining a household is so great that young men are afraid to marry, — and that it costs more now per annum to dress one young woman than it used to cost to carry a whole family of sons through college. In short, the poor old gentleman is in a desperate state of mind, and is firmly of opinion that society is going to ruin by an express train."

"Poor old fellow!" said I, "the only comfort I can offer him is what I take myself, — that this sad world will last out our time at least. Now for the next."

"The next is more concise and spicy," said my wife. "I will read it.

" ' *Christopher Crowfield, Esq.,*

" ' SIR, — If you want to know how American women are to be brought back to family work, I can tell you a short method. Pay them as good wages for it as they can make in any other way. I get from seven to nine dollars a week in the shop where I work; if I could make the same in any good family, I should have no objection to doing it.

" ' Your obedient servant,

" ' LETITIA.' "

"My correspondent Letitia does not tell me," said I, "how much of this seven or nine dollars she pays out for board and washing, fire and lights. If she worked in a good family at two or three dollars a week, it is easily demonstrable, that, at the present cost of these items, she would make as much clear profit as she now does at nine dollars for her shop-work.

" And there are two other things, moreover, which she does not consider : First, that, besides board, washing, fuel, and lights, which she would have in a family, she would have also less unintermitted toil. Shop-work exacts its ten hours per diem ; and it makes no allowance for sickness or accident.

" A good domestic in a good family finds many hours when she can feel free to attend to her own affairs. Her work consists of certain definite matters, which being done her time is her own ; and if she have skill and address in the management of her duties, she may secure many leisure hours. As houses are now built, and with the many labor-saving conveniences that are being introduced, the physical labor of housework is no more than a healthy woman really needs to keep her in health. In case, however, of those slight illnesses to which all are more or less liable, and which, if neglected, often lead to graver ones, the advantage is still on the side of domestic service. In the shop and factory, every hour of un-employed time is deducted ; an illness of a day or two is an appreciable loss of just so much money, while the expense of board is still going on. But in the family a good servant is always considered. When ill, she is carefully nursed as one of the family, has the family physician, and is subject to no deduction from her wages for loss of time. I have known more than one instance in which a valued domestic has been sent, at her employer's expense, to the seaside or some other pleasant locality, for change of air, when her health has been run down.

"In the second place, family work is more remunerative, even at a lower rate of wages, than shop or factory work, because it is better for the health. All sorts of sedentary employment, pursued by numbers of persons together in one apartment, are more or less debilitating and unhealthy, through foul air and confinement.

"A woman's health is her capital. In certain ways of work she obtains more income, but she spends on her capital to do it. In another way she may get less income, and yet increase her capital. A woman cannot work at dress-making, tailoring, or any other sedentary employment, ten hours a day, year in and out, without enfeebling her constitution, impairing her eyesight, and bringing on a complication of complaints, but she can sweep, wash, cook, and do the varied duties of a well-ordered house with modern arrangements, and grow healthier every year. The times, in New England, when all women did housework a part of every day, were the times when all women were healthy. At present, the heritage of vigorous muscles, firm nerves, strong backs, and cheerful physical life has gone from American women, and is taken up by Irish women. A thrifty young man, I have lately heard of, married a rosy young Irish girl, quite to the horror of his mother and sisters, but defended himself by the following very conclusive logic : 'If I marry an American girl, I must have an Irish girl to take care of her ; and I cannot afford to support both.'

" Besides all this, there is a third consideration, which I humbly commend to my friend Letitia. The turn of her note speaks her a girl of good common sense, with a faculty of hitting the nail square on the head ; and such a girl must see that nothing is more likely to fall out than that she will some day be married. Evidently, our fair friend is born to rule ; and at this hour, doubtless, her foreordained throne and humble servant are somewhere awaiting her.

" Now domestic service is all the while fitting a girl physically, mentally, and morally for her ultimate vocation and sphere, — to be a happy wife and to make a happy home. But factory work, shop work, and all employments of that sort, are in their nature essentially *undomestic*, — entailing the constant necessity of a boarding-house life, and of habits as different as possible from the quiet routine of home. The girl who is ten hours on the strain of continued, unintermitted toil feels no inclination, when evening comes, to sit down and darn her stockings, or make over her dresses, or study any of those multifarious economies which turn a wardrobe to the best account. Her nervous system is flagging; she craves company and excitement; and her dull, narrow room is deserted for some place of amusement or gay street promenade. And who can blame her? Let any sensible woman, who has had experience of shop and factory life, recall to her mind the ways and manners in which young girls grow up who leave a father's roof for a crowded boarding-house, without any supervision of matron or mother, and ask whether this is the best school for training young American wives and mothers.

"Doubtless there are discreet and thoughtful women who, amid all these difficulties, do keep up thrifty, womanly habits, but they do it by an effort greater than the majority of girls are willing to make, and greater than they ought to make. To sew or read or study after ten hours of factory or shop work is a further drain on the nervous powers, which no woman can long endure without exhaustion.

"When the time arrives that such a girl comes to a house of her own, she comes to it as unskilled in all household lore, with muscles as incapable of domestic labor, and nerves as sensitive, as if she had been leading the most luxurious, do-nothing, fashionable life. How different would be her preparation, had the forming years of her life been spent in the labors of a family! I know at this moment a lady at the head of a rich country establishment, filling her station in society with dignity and honor, who gained her domestic education in a kitchen in our vicinity. She was the daughter of a small farmer, and when the time came for her to be earning her living, her parents wisely thought it far better that she should gain it in a way which would at the same time establish her health and fit her for her own future home. In a cheerful, light, airy kitchen, which was kept so tidy always as to be an attractive sitting-room, she and another young country-girl were trained up in the best of domestic economies by a mistress who looked well to the ways of her household, till at length they married from the house with honor, and went to practise in homes of their own the lessons they had learned in the home of another. Formerly, in New England, such instances were not uncommon; — would that they might become so again!"

"The fact is," said my wife, "the places which the daughters of American farmers used to occupy in our families are now taken by young girls from the families of small farmers in Ireland. They are respectable, tidy, healthy, and capable of being taught. A good mistress, who is reasonable and liberal in her treatment, is able to make them fixtures. They get good wages, and have few expenses. They dress handsomely, have abundant leisure to take care of their clothes and turn their wardrobes to the best account, and they very soon acquire skill in doing it equal to that displayed by any women of any country. They remit money continually to relatives in Ireland, and from time to time pay the passage of one and another to this country, — and whole families have thus been established in American life by the efforts of one young girl. Now, for my part, I do not grudge my Irish fellow-citizens these advantages obtained by honest labor and good conduct; they deserve all the good fortune thus accruing to them. But when I see sickly, nervous American women jostling and struggling in the few crowded avenues which are open to mere brain, I cannot help thinking how much better their lot would have been, with good strong bodies, steady nerves, healthy digestion, and the habit of looking any kind of work in the face, which used to be characteristic of American women generally, and of Yankee women in particular."

"The matter becomes still graver," said I, "by the laws of descent. The woman who enfeebles her muscular system by sedentary occupation, and over-stimulates her brain and nervous system, when she becomes a mother, perpetuates these evils to her offspring. Her children will be born feeble and deli cate, incapable of sustaining any severe strain of body or mind. The universal cry now about the ill health of young American girls is the fruit of some three generations of neglect of physical exercise and undue stimulus of brain and nerves. Young girls now are universally *born* delicate. The most careful hygienic treatment during childhood, the strictest attention to diet, dress, and exercise, succeeds merely so far as to produce a girl who is healthy so long only as she does nothing. With the least strain, her delicate organism gives out, now here, now there. She can not study without her eyes fail or she has headache, — she cannot get up her own muslins, or sweep a room, or pack a trunk, without bringing on a backache, — she goes to a concert or a lecture, and must lie by all the next day from the exertion. If she skates, she is sure to strain some muscle ; or if she falls and strikes her knee or hits her ankle, a blow that a healthy girl would forget in five minutes terminates in some mysterious lameness which confines our poor sibyl for months.

" The young American girl of our times is a creature who has not a particle of vitality to spare, — no reserved stock of force to draw upon in cases of family exigency. She is exquisitely strung, she is cultivated, she is refined ; but she is too nervous, too wiry, too sensitive, — she burns away too fast; only the easiest of circumstances, the most watchful of care and nursing, can keep her within the limits of comfortable health ; and yet this is the creature who must undertake family life in a country where it is next to an absolute impossibility to have *permanent* domestics. Frequent change, occasional entire break-downs, must be the lot of the majority of housekeep-ers, — particularly those who do not live in cities."

"In fact," said my wife, "we in America have so far got out of the way of a womanhood that has any vigor of outline or opulence of physical proportions, that, when we see a woman made as a woman ought to be, she strikes us as a monster. Our willowy girls are afraid of nothing so much as growing stout ; and if a young lady begins to round into proportions like the women in Titian's and Giorgione's pictures, she is distressed above measure, and begins to make secret inquiries into reducing diet, and to cling des-perately to the strongest corset-lacing as her only hope. It would require one to be better educated than most of our girls are, to be willing to look like the Sistine Madonna or the Venus of Milo.

"Once in a while our Italian opera-singers bring to our shores those glorious physiques which formed the inspiration of Italian painters ; and then American editors make coarse jokes about Barnum's fat woman, and avalanches, and pretend to be struck with terror at such dimensions.

"We should be better instructed, and consider that Italy does us a favor, in sending us specimens, not only of higher styles of musical art, but of a warmer, richer, and more abundant womanly life. The magnificent voice is only in keeping with the magnificent proportions of the singer. A voice which has no grate, no strain, which flows without effort, — which does not labor eagerly up to a high note, but alights on it like a bird from above, there carelessly warbling and trilling, — a voice which then without effort sinks into broad, rich, sombre depths of soft, heavy chest-tone, — can come only with a physical nature at once strong, wide, and fine, — from a nature such as the sun of Italy ripens, as he does her golden grapes, filling it with the new wine of song."

"Well," said I, "so much for our strictures on Miss Letitia's letter. What comes next?"

"Here is a correspondent who answers the question, 'What shall we do with her?' — *apropos* to the case of the distressed young woman which we considered in our first chapter."

"And what does he recommend?"

"He tells us that *he* should advise us to make our distressed woman Marianne's housekeeper, and to send South for three or four contrabands for her to train, and, with great apparent complacency, seems to think that course will solve all similar cases of difficulty."

"That's quite a man's view of the subject," said Jennie. "They think any woman who is n't particularly fitted to do anything else can keep house."

"As if housekeeping were not the very highest craft and mystery of social life," said I. "I admit that our sex speak too unadvisedly on such topics, and, being well instructed by my household priestesses, will humbly suggest the following ideas to my correspondent.

"1st. A woman is not of course fit to be a housekeeper because she is a woman of good education and refinement.

"2d. If she were, a family with young children in it is not the proper place to establish a school for untaught contrabands, however desirable their training may be.

"A woman of good education and good common sense may *learn* to be a good housekeeper, as she learns any trade, by going into a good family and practising first one and then another branch of the business, till finally she shall acquire the comprehensive knowedge to direct all.

"The next letter I will read.

"'DEAR MR. CROWFIELD, — Your papers relating to the domestic problem have touched upon a difficulty which threatens to become a matter of life and death with me.

" 'I am a young man, with good health, good courage, and good prospects. I have, for a young man, a fair income, and a prospect of its increase. But my business requires me to reside in a country town near a great manufacturing city. The demand for labor there has made such a drain on the female population of the vicinity, that it seems, for a great part of the time, impossible to keep any servants at all ; and what we can hire are of the poorest quality, and want exorbitant wages. My wife was a well-trained housekeeper, and knows perfectly all that pertains to the care of a family ; but she has three little children, and a delicate babe only a few weeks old ; and *can* any one woman do all that is needed for such a household ? Something must be trusted to servants ; and what is thus trusted brings such con-fusion and waste and dirt into our house, that the poor woman is constantly distraught between the disgust of having them and the utter impossibility of doing without them.

" 'Now it has been suggested that we remedy the trouble by paying higher wages ; but I find that for the very highest wages I secure only the most mis-erable service ; and yet, poor as it is, we are obliged to put up with it, because there is an amount of work to be done in our family that is absolutely beyond my wife's strength.

" ' I see her health wearing away under these trials, her life made a burden ; I feel no power to help her ; and I ask you, Mr. Crowfield, What are we to do ? What is to become of family life in this country ?

" ' Yours truly,

" ' A YOUNG FAMILY MAN.'

"My friend's letter," said I, "touches upon the very hinge of the difficulty of domestic life with the present generation.

" The real, vital difficulty, after all, in our American life is, that our country is so wide, so various, so abounding in the richest fields of enterprise, that in every direction the cry is of the plenteousness of the harvest and the fewness of the laborers. In short, there really are not laborers enough to do the work of the country.

" Since the war has thrown the whole South open to the competition of free labor, the demand for workers is doubled and trebled. Manufactories of all sorts are enlarging their borders, increasing their machinery, and calling for more hands. Every article of living is demanded with an imperativeness and over an extent of territory which set at once additional thousands to the task of production. Instead of being easier to find hands to execute in all branches of useful labor, it is likely to grow every year more difficult, as new departments of manufacture and trade divide the workers. The price of labor, even now higher in this country than in any other, will rise still higher, and thus complicate still more the problem of domestic life. Even if a reasonable quota of intelligent women choose domestic service, the demand will be increasingly beyond the supply."

"And what have you to say to this," said my wife, "seeing you cannot stop the prosperity of the country?"

"Simply this, — that communities will be driven to organize, as they now do in Europe, to lessen the labors of individual families by having some of the present domestic tasks done out of the house.

"In France, for example, no housekeeper counts either washing, ironing, or bread-making as part of her domestic cares. All the family washing goes out to a laundry; and being attended to by those who make that department of labor a specialty, it comes home in refreshingly beautiful order.

"We in America, though we pride ourselves on our Yankee thrift, are far behind the French in domestic economy. If all the families of a neighborhood should put together the sums they separately spend in buying or fitting up and keeping in repair tubs, boilers, and other accommodations for washing, all that is consumed or wasted in soap, starch, bluing, fuel, together with the wages and board of an extra servant, the aggregate would suffice to fit up a neighborhood laundry, where one or two capable women could do easily and well what ten or fifteen women now do painfully and ill, and to the confusion and derangement of all other family processes.

"The model laundries for the poor in London had facilities which would enable a woman to do both the washing and ironing of a small family in from two to three hours, and were so arranged that a very few women could with ease do the work of the neighborhood.

"But in the absence of an establishment of this sort, the housekeepers of a country village might help themselves very much by owning a mangle in common, to which all the heavier parts of the ironing could be sent. American ingenuity has greatly improved the machinery of the mangle. It is no longer the heavy, cumbersome structure that it used to be in the Old World, but a compact, neat piece of apparatus, made in three or four different sizes to suit different-sized apartments.

"Mr. H. F. Bond of Waltham, Massachusetts, now manufactures these articles, and sends them to all parts of the country. The smallest of them does not take up much more room than a sewing-machine, can be turned by a boy of ten or twelve, and thus in the course of an hour or two the heaviest and most fatiguing part of a family ironing may be accomplished.

" I should certainly advise the ' Young Family Man' with a delicate wife and uncertain domestic help to fortify his kitchen with one of these fixtures.

" But after all, I still say that the quarter to which I look for the solution of the American problem of domestic life is a wise use of the principle of association.

" The future model village of New England, as I see it, shall have for the use of its inhabitants not merely a town lyceum-hall and a town library, but a town laundry, fitted up with conveniences such as no private house can afford, and paying a price to the operators which will enable them to command an excellence of work such as private families seldom realize. It will also have a town bakery, where the best of family bread, white, brown, and of all grains, shall be compounded ; and lastly a town cook-shop, where soup and meats may be bought, ready for the table. Those of us who have kept house abroad remember the ease with which our foreign establishments were carried on. A suite of elegant apartments, a courier, and one female servant, were the foundation of domestic life. Our courier boarded us at a moderate expense, and the servant took care of our rooms. Punctually to the dinner-hour every day, our dinner came in on the head of a porter from a neighboring cook-shop. A large chest lined with tin, and kept warm by a tiny charcoal stove in the centre, being deposited in an ante-room, from it came forth, first, soup, then fish, then roast of various names, and lastly pastry and confections, — far more courses than any reasonable Christian needs to keep him in healthy condition; and dinner being over, our box with its *débris* went out of the house, leaving a clear field.

"Now I put it to the distressed 'Young Family Man' whether these three institutions of a bakery, a cook-shop, and a laundry, in the village where he lives, would not virtually annihilate his household cares, and restore peace and comfort to his now distracted family.

"There really is no more reason why every family should make its own bread than its own butter, — why every family should do its own washing and iron-ing than its own tailoring or mantua-making. In France, where certainly the arts of economy are well studied, there is some specialty for many domestic needs for which we keep servants. The beautiful in-laid floors are kept waxed and glossy by a professional gentleman who wears a brush on his foot-sole, skates gracefully over the surface, and, leaving all right, de-parteth. Many families, each paying a small sum, keep this servant in common.

" Now if ever there was a community which needed to study the art of living, it is our American one ; for at present, domestic life is so wearing and so oppressive as seriously to affect health and happiness. Whatever has been done abroad in the way of comfort and convenience can be done here ; and the first neighborhood that shall set the example of dividing the tasks and burdens of life by the judicious use of the principle of *association* will initiate a most important step in the way of national happiness and prosperity.

" My solution, then, of the domestic problem may be formulized as follows : —

" 1st. That women make self-helpfulness and family helpfulness fashionable, and every woman use her muscles daily in enough household work to give her a good digestion.

" 2d. That the situation of a domestic be made so respectable and respected that well-educated American women shall be induced to take it as a training-school for their future family life.

" 3d. That families by association lighten the multifarious labors of the domestic sphere.

" All of which I humbly submit to the good sense and enterprise of American readers and workers."

VI.

BODILY RELIGION: A SERMON ON GOOD HEALTH.

ONE of our recent writers has said, that "good health is physical religion"; and it is a saying worthy to be printed in golden letters. But good health being physical religion, it fully shares that indifference with which the human race regards things confessedly the most important. The neglect of the soul is the trite theme of all religious teachers; and, next to their souls, there is nothing that people neglect so much as their bodies. Every person ought to be perfectly healthy, just as everybody ought to be perfectly religious; but, in point of fact, the greater part of mankind are so far from perfect moral or physical religion that they cannot even form a conception of the blessing beyond them.

The mass of good, well-meaning Christians are not yet advanced enough to guess at the change which a perfect fidelity to Christ's spirit and precepts would produce in them. And the majority of people who

call themselves well, because they are not, at present,
upon any particular doctor's list, are not within sight
of what perfect health would be. That fulness of life,
that vigorous tone, and that elastic cheerfulness, which
make the mere fact of existence a luxury, that supple-
ness which carries one like a well-built boat over
every wave of unfavorable chance, — these are attributes of the perfect health seldom enjoyed. We see
them in young children, in animals, and now and
then, but rarely, in some adult human being, who has
preserved intact the religion of the body through
all opposing influences. Perfect health supposes
not a state of mere quiescence, but of positive
enjoyment in living. See that little fellow, as his
nurse turns him out in the morning, fresh from his
bath, his hair newly curled, and his cheeks polished
like apples. Every step is a spring or a dance ; he
runs, he laughs, he shouts, his face breaks into a thousand dimpling smiles at a word. His breakfast of
plain bread and milk is swallowed with an eager and
incredible delight, — it is *so good* that he stops to
laugh or thump the table now and then in expression
of his ecstasy. All day long he runs and frisks and
plays ; and when at night the little head seeks the
pillow, down go the eye-curtains, and sleep comes
without a dream. In the morning his first note is a
laugh and a crow, as he sits up in his crib and tries

to pull papa's eyes open with his fat fingers. He is an embodied joy,— he is sunshine and music and laughter for all the house. With what a magnificent generosity does the Author of life endow a little mortal pilgrim in giving him at the outset of his career such a body as this! How miserable it is to look forward twenty years, when the same child, now grown a man, wakes in the morning with a dull, heavy head, the consequence of smoking and studying till twelve or one the night before; when he rises languidly to a late breakfast, and turns from this, and tries that,— wants a devilled bone, or a cutlet with Worcestershire sauce, to make eating possible; and then, with slow and plodding step, finds his way to his office and his books. Verily the shades of the prison-house gather round the growing boy; for, surely, no one will deny that life often begins with health little less perfect than that of the angels.

But the man who habitually wakes sodden, headachy, and a little stupid, and who needs a cup of strong coffee and various stimulating condiments to coax his bodily system into something like fair working order, does not suppose he is out of health. He says, "Very well, I thank you," to your inquiries,— merely because he has entirely forgotten what good health is. He is well, not because of any particular pleasure in physical existence, but well simply because he is not a subject for prescriptions. Yet there is no store of vitality, no buoyancy, no superabundant vigor, to resist the strain and pressure to which life puts him. A checked perspiration, a draught of air ill-timed, a crisis of perplexing business or care, and he is down with a bilious attack, or an influenza, and subject to doctors' orders for an indefinite period. And if the case be so with men, how is it with wo men? How many women have at maturity the keen appetite, the joyous love of life and motion, the elasticity and sense of physical delight in existence, that little children have? How many have any superabundance of vitality with which to meet the wear and strain of life? And yet they call themselves well.

But is it possible, in maturity, to have the joyful fulness of the life of childhood? Experience has shown that the delicious freshness of this dawning hour may be preserved even to mid-day, and may be brought back and restored after it has been for years a stranger. Nature, though a severe disciplinarian, is still, in many respects, most patient and easy to be entreated, and meets any repentant movement of her prodigal children with wonderful condescension. Take Bulwer's account of the first few weeks of his sojourn at Malvern, and you will read, in very elegant English, the story of an experience of pleasure which has surprised and delighted many a patient at a water-

7   1

cure. The return to the great primitive elements of health — water, air, and simple food, with a regular system of exercise — has brought to many a jaded, weary, worn-down human being the elastic spirits, the simple, eager appetite, the sound sleep, of a little child. Hence, the rude huts and châlets of the peasant Priessnitz were crowded with battered dukes and princesses, and notables of every degree, who came from the hot, enervating luxury which had drained them of existence to find a keener pleasure in peasants' bread under peasants' roofs than in soft raiment and palaces. No arts of French cookery can possibly make anything taste so well to a feeble and palled appetite as plain brown bread and milk taste to a hungry water-cure patient, fresh from bath and exercise.

If the water-cure had done nothing more than establish the fact that the glow and joyousness of early life are things which may be restored after having been once wasted, it would have done a good work. For if Nature is so forgiving to those who have once lost or have squandered her treasures, what may not be hoped for us if we can learn the art of never losing the first health of childhood? And though with us, who have passed to maturity, it may be too late for the blessing, cannot something be done for the children who are yet to come after us?

Why is the first health of childhood lost? Is it not the answer, that childhood is the only period of life in which bodily health is made a prominent object? Take our pretty boy, with cheeks like apples, who started in life with a hop, skip, and dance, — to whom laughter was like breathing, and who was enraptured with plain bread and milk, — how did he grow into the man who wakes so languid and dull, who wants strong coffee and Worcestershire sauce to make his breakfast go down? When and where did he drop the invaluable talisman that once made everything look brighter and taste better to him, however rude and simple, than now do the most elaborate combinations? What is the boy's history? Why, for the first seven years of his life his body is made of some account. It is watched, cared for, dieted, disciplined, fed with fresh air, and left to grow and develop like a thrifty plant. But from the time school education begins, the body is steadily ignored, and left to take care of itself.

The boy is made to sit six hours a day in a close, hot room, breathing impure air, putting the brain and the nervous system upon a constant strain, while the muscular system is repressed to an unnatural quiet. During the six hours, perhaps twenty minutes are allowed for all that play of the muscles which, up to this time, has been the constant habit of his life.

After this he is sent home with books, slate, and lessons to occupy an hour or two more in preparing for the next day. In the whole of this time there is no kind of effort to train the physical system by appropriate exercise. Something of the sort was attempted years ago in the infant schools, but soon given up; and now, from the time study first begins, the muscles are ignored in all primary schools. One of the first results is the loss of that animal vigor which formerly made the boy love motion for its own sake. Even in his leisure hours he no longer leaps and runs as he used to; he learns to sit still, and by and by sitting and lounging come to be the habit, and vigorous motion the exception, for most of the hours of the day. The education thus begun goes on from primary to high school, from high school to college, from college through professional studies of law, medicine, or theology, with this steady contempt for the body, with no provision for its culture, training, or development, but rather a direct and evident provision for its deterioration and decay.

The want of suitable ventilation in school-rooms, recitation-rooms, lecture-rooms, offices, court-rooms, conference-rooms, and vestries, where young students of law, medicine, and theology acquire 'their earlier practice, is something simply appalling. Of itself it would answei for men the question, why so many

thousand glad, active children come to a middle life
without joy, — a life whose best estate is a sort of
slow, plodding endurance. The despite and hatred
which most men seem to feel for God's gift of fresh
air, and their resolution to breathe as little of it as
possible, could only come from a long course of education, in which they have been accustomed to live
without it. Let any one notice the conduct of our
American people travelling in railroad cars. We will
suppose that about half of them are what might be
called well-educated people, who have learned in
books, or otherwise, that the air breathed from the
lungs is laden with impurities, — that it is noxious
and poisonous ; and yet, travel with these people half
a day, and you would suppose from their actions that
they considered the external air as a poison created
expressly to injure them, and that the only course of
safety lay in keeping the cars hermetically sealed, and
breathing over and over the vapor from each others'
lungs. If a person in despair at the intolerable foul-
ness raises a window, what frowns from all the neighboring seats, especially from great rough-coated men,
who always seem the first to be apprehensive ! The
request to "put down that window" is almost sure to
follow a moment or two of fresh air. In vain have
rows of ventilators been put in the tops of some of the
cars, for conductors and passengers are both of one

mind, that these ventilators are inlets of danger, and must be kept carefully closed.

Railroad travelling in America is systematically, and one would think carefully, arranged so as to violate every possible law of health. The old rule to keep the head cool and the feet warm is precisely reversed. A red-hot stove heats the upper stratum of air to oppression, while a stream of cold air is constantly circulating about the lower extremities. The most indigestible and unhealthy substances conceivable are generally sold in the cars or at way-stations for the confusion and distress of the stomach. Rarely can a traveller obtain so innocent a thing as a plain good sandwich of bread and meat, while pie, cake, doughnuts, and all other culinary atrocities, are almost forced upon him at every stopping-place. In France, England, and Germany the railroad cars are perfectly ventilated ; the feet are kept warm by flat cases filled with hot water and covered with carpet, and answering the double purpose of warming the feet and diffusing an agreeable temperature through the car, without burning away the vitality of the air ; while the arrangements at the refreshment-rooms provide for the passenger as wholesome and well-served a meal of healthy, nutritious food as could be obtained in any home circle.

What are we to infer concerning the home habits

of a nation of men who so resignedly allow their bodies to be poisoned and maltreated in travelling over such an extent of territory as is covered by our railroad lines? Does it not show that foul air and improper food are too much matters of course to excite attention? As a writer in "The Nation" has lately remarked, it is simply and only because the American nation like to have unventilated cars, and to be fed on pie and coffee at stopping-places, that nothing better is known to our travellers; if there were any marked dislike of such a state of things on the part of the people, it would not exist. We have wealth enough, and enterprise enough, and ingenuity enough, in our American nation, to compass with wonderful rapidity any end that really seems to us desirable. An army was improvised when an army was wanted, — and an army more perfectly equipped, more bountifully fed, than so great a body of men ever was before. Hospitals, Sanitary Commissions, and Christian Commissions all arose out of the simple conviction of the American people that they must arise. If the American people were equally convinced that foul air was a poison, — that to have cold feet and hot heads was to invite an attack of illness, — that maple-sugar, pop-corn, peppermint candy, pie, doughnuts, and peanuts are not diet for reasonable beings, — they would have railroad accommodations very different from those now in existence.

We have spoken of the foul air of court-rooms. What better illustration could be given of the utter contempt with which the laws of bodily health are treated, than the condition of these places? Our lawyers are our highly educated men. They have been through high-school and college training, they have learned the properties of oxygen, nitrogen, and carbonic-acid gas, and have seen a mouse die under an exhausted receiver, and of course they know that foul, unventilated rooms are bad for the health; and yet generation after generation of men so taught and trained will spend the greater part of their lives in rooms notorious for their close and impure air, without so much as an attempt to remedy the evil. A well-ventilated court-room is a four-leaved clover among court-rooms. Young men are constantly losing their health at the bar; lung diseases, dyspepsia, follow them up, gradually sapping their vitality. Some of the brightest ornaments of the profession have actually fallen dead as they stood pleading, — victims of the fearful pressure of poisonous and heated air upon the excited brain. The deaths of Salmon P. Chase of Portland, uncle of our present Chief Justice, and of Ezekiel Webster, the brother of our great statesman, are memorable examples of the calamitous effects of the errors dwelt upon; and yet, strange to say, nothing efficient is done to mend these errors, and give the body an equal chance with the mind in the pressure of the world's affairs.

But churches, lecture-rooms, and vestries, and all buildings devoted especially to the good of the soul, are equally witness of the mind's disdain of the body's needs, and the body's consequent revenge upon the soul. In how many of these places has the question of a thorough provision of fresh air been even considered? People would never think of bringing a thousand persons into a desert place, and keeping them there, without making preparations to feed them. Bread and butter, potatoes and meat, must plainly be found for them ; but a thousand human beings are put into a building to remain a given number of hours, and no one asks the question whether means exist for giving each one the quantum of fresh air needed for his circulation, and these thousand victims will consent to be slowly poisoned, gasping, sweating, getting red in the face, with confused and sleepy brains, while a minister with a yet redder face and a more oppressed brain struggles and wrestles, through the hot, seething vapors, to make clear to them the mysteries of faith. How many churches are there that for six or eight months in the year are never ventilated at all, except by the accidental opening of doors? The foul air generated by one congregation is locked up by the sexton for the use of the next

7*

assembly ; and so gathers and gathers from week to week, and month to month, while devout persons upbraid themselves, and are ready to tear their hair, because they always feel stupid and sleepy in church. The proper ventilation of their churches and vestries would remove that spiritual deadness of which their prayers and hymns complain. A man hoeing his corn out on a breezy hillside is bright and alert, his mind works clearly, and he feels interested in religion, and thinks of many a thing that might be said at the prayer-meeting at night. But at night, when he sits down in a little room where the air reeks with the vapor of his neighbor's breath and the smoke of kerosene lamps, he finds himself suddenly dull and drowsy, — without emotion, without thought, without feeling, — and he rises and reproaches himself for this state of things. He calls upon his soul and all that is within him to bless the Lord ; but the indignant body, abused, insulted, ignored, takes the soul by the throat, and says, "If you won't let *me* have a good time, neither shall you." Revivals of religion, with ministers and with those people whose moral organization leads them to take most interest in them, often end in periods of bodily ill-health and depression. But is there any need of this? Suppose that a revival of religion required, as a formula, that all the members of a given congregation should daily take a minute dose of arsenic in concert, — we should not be surprised after a while to hear of various ill effects therefrom ; and, as vestries and lecture-rooms are now arranged, a daily prayer-meeting is often nothing more nor less than a number of persons spending half an hour a day breathing poison from each other's lungs. There is not only no need of this, but, on the contrary, a good supply of pure air would make the daily prayer-meeting far more enjoyable. The body, if allowed the slighest degree of fair play, so far from being a contumacious infidel and opposer, becomes a very fair Christian helper, and, instead of throttling the soul, gives it wings to rise to celestial regions.

This branch of our subject we will quit with one significant anecdote. A certain rural church was somewhat famous for its picturesque Gothic architecture, and equally famous for its sleepy atmosphere, the rules of Gothic symmetry requiring very small windows, which could be only partially opened. Everybody was affected alike in this church ; minister and people complained that it was like the enchanted ground in the Pilgrim's Progress. Do what they would, sleep was ever at their elbows ; the blue, red, and green of the painted windows melted into a rainbow dimness of hazy confusion ; and ere they were aware, they were off on a cloud to the land of dreams.

An energetic sister in the church suggested the inquiry, whether it was ever ventilated, and discovered that it was regularly locked up at the close of service, and remained so till opened for the next week. She suggested the inquiry, whether giving the church a thorough airing on Saturday would not improve the Sunday services; but nobody acted on her suggestion. Finally, she borrowed the sexton's key one Saturday night, and went into the church and opened all the windows herself, and let them remain so for the night. The next day everybody remarked the improved comfort of the church, and wondered what had produced the change. Nevertheless, when it was discovered, it was not deemed a matter of enough importance to call for an order on the sexton to perpetuate the improvement.

The ventilation of private dwellings in this country is such as might be expected from that entire indifference to the laws of health manifested in public establishments. Let a person travel in private conveyance up through the valley of the Connecticut, and stop for a night at the taverns which he will usually find at the end of each day's stage. The bed-chamber into which he will be ushered will be the concentration of all forms of bad air. The house is redolent of the vegetables in the cellar, — cabbages, turnips, and potatoes; and this fragrance is confined and retained by the custom of closing the window-blinds and dropping the inside curtains, so that neither air nor sunshine enters in to purify. Add to this the strong odor of a new feather-bed and pillows, and you have a combination of perfumes most appalling to a delicate sense. Yet travellers take possession of these rooms, sleep in them all night without raising the window or opening the blinds, and leave them to be shut up for other travellers.

The spare chamber of many dwellings seems to be an hermetically closed box, opened only twice a year, for spring and fall cleaning; but for the rest of the time closed to the sun and the air of heaven. Thrifty country housekeepers often adopt the custom of making their beds on the instant after they are left, without airing the sheets and mattresses; and a bed so made gradually becomes permeated with the insensible emanations of the human body, so as to be a steady corrupter of the atmosphere.

In the winter, the windows are calked and listed, the throat of the chimney built up with a tight brick wall, and a close stove is introduced to help burn out the vitality of the air. In a sitting-room like this, from five to ten persons will spend about eight months of the year, with no other ventilation than that gained by the casual opening and shutting of doors. Is it any wonder that consumption every year sweeps away its thousands? — that people are suffering constant chronic ailments, — neuralgia, nervous dyspepsia, and all the host of indefinite bad feelings that rob life of sweetness and flower and bloom?

A recent writer raises the inquiry, whether the community would not gain in health by the demolition of all dwelling-houses. That is, he suggests the question, whether the evils from foul air are not so great and so constant, that they countervail the advantages of shelter. Consumptive patients far gone have been known to be cured by long journeys, which have required them to be day and night in the open air. Sleep under the open heaven, even though the person be exposed to the various accidents of weather, has often proved a miraculous restorer after everything else had failed. But surely, if simple fresh air is so healing and preserving a thing, some means might be found to keep the air in a house just as pure and vigorous as it is outside.

An article in the May number of "Harpers' Magazine" presents drawings of a very simple arrangement by which any house can be made thoroughly self-ventilating. Ventilation, as this article shows, consists in two things, — a perfect and certain expulsion from the dwelling of all foul air breathed from the lungs or arising from any other cause, and the constant supply of pure air.

One source of foul air cannot be too much guarded against, — we mean imperfect gas-pipes. A want of thoroughness in execution is the sin of our American artisans, and very few gas-fixtures are so thoroughly made that more or less gas does not escape and mingle with the air of the dwelling. There are parlors where plants cannot be made to live, because the gas kills them ; and yet their occupants do not seem to reflect that an air in which a plant cannot live must be dangerous for a human being. The very clemency and long-suffering of Nature to those who persistently violate her laws is one great cause why men are, physically speaking, such sinners as they are. If foul air poisoned at once and completely, we should have well-ventilated houses, whatever else we failed to have. But because people can go on for weeks, months, and years, breathing poisons, and slowly and imperceptibly lowering the tone of their vital powers, and yet be what they call " pretty well, I thank you," sermons on ventilation and fresh air go by them as an idle song. " I don't see but we are well enough, and we never took much pains about these things. There 's air enough gets into houses, of course. What with doors opening and windows occasionally lifted, the air of houses is generally good enough " ; — and so the matter is dismissed.

One of Heaven's great hygienic teachers is now

abroad in the world, giving lessons on health to the children of men. The cholera is like the angel whom God threatened to send as leader to the rebellious Israelites. "Beware of him, obey his voice, and provoke him not; for he will not pardon your transgressions." The advent of this fearful messenger seems really to be made necessary by the contempt with which men treat the physical laws of their being. What else could have purified the dark places of New York? What a wiping-up and reforming and cleansing is going before him through the country! At last we find that Nature is in earnest, and that her laws cannot be always ignored with impunity. Poisoned air is recognized at last as an evil, — even although the poison cannot be weighed, measured, or tasted; and if all the precautions that men are now willing to take could be made perpetual, the alarm would be a blessing to the world.

Like the principles of spiritual religion, the principles of physical religion are few and easy to be understood. An old medical apothegm personifies the hygienic forces as the Doctors Air, Diet, Exercise, and Quiet; and these four will be found, on reflection, to cover the whole ground of what is required to preserve human health. A human being whose lungs have always been nourished by pure air, whose stomach has been fed only by appropriate food, whose

muscles have been systematically trained by appropriate exercises, and whose mind is kept tranquil by
faith in God and a good conscience, has *perfect physical religion.* There is a line where physical religion
must necessarily overlap spiritual religion and rest
upon it. No human being can be assured of perfect
health, through all the strain and wear and tear of
such cares and such perplexities as life brings, without
the rest of *faith in God.* An unsubmissive, unconfid-
ing, unresigned soul will make vain the best hygienic
treatment; and, on the contrary, the most saintly religious resolution and purpose may be defeated and
vitiated by an habitual ignorance and disregard of the
laws of the physical system.

Perfect spiritual religion cannot exist without perfect
physical religion. Every flaw and defect in the bodily
system is just so much taken from the spiritual vitality: we are commanded to glorify God, not simply in
our spirits, but in our *bodies* and spirits. The only
example of perfect manhood the world ever saw im-
presses us more than anything else by an atmosphere
of perfect healthiness. There is a calmness, a steadiness, in the character of Jesus, a naturalness in his
evolution of the sublimest truths under the strain of
the most absorbing and intense excitement, that could
come only from the *one* perfectly trained and developed body, bearing as a pure and sacred shrine the

K

One Perfect Spirit. Jesus of Nazareth, journeying on foot from city to city, always calm yet always fervent, always steady yet glowing with a white heat of sacred enthusiasm, able to walk and teach all day and afterwards to continue in prayer all night, with unshaken nerves, sedately patient, serenely reticent, perfectly self-controlled, walked the earth, the only man that perfectly glorified God in his body no less than in his spirit. It is worthy of remark, that in choosing his disciples he chose plain men from the laboring classes, who had lived the most obediently to the simple, unperverted laws of nature. He chose men of good and pure bodies, — simple, natural, childlike, healthy men, — and baptized their souls with the inspiration of the Holy Spirit.

The hygienic bearings of the New Testament have never been sufficiently understood. The basis of them lies in the solemn declaration, that our bodies are to be temples of the Holy Spirit, and that all abuse of them is of the nature of sacrilege. Reverence for the physical system, as the outward shrine and temple of the spiritual, is the peculiarity of the Christian religion. The doctrine of the resurrection of the body, and its physical immortality, sets the last crown of honor upon it. That bodily system which God declared worthy to be gathered back from the dust of the grave, and re-created, as the soul's immor tal companion, must necessarily be dear and precious in the eyes of its Creator. The one passage in the New Testament in which it is spoken of disparagingly is where Paul contrasts it with the brighter glory of what is to come : " He shall change our *vile* bodies, that they may be fashioned like his glorious body." From this passage has come abundance of reviling of the physical system. Memoirs of good men are full of abuse of it, as the clog, the load, the burden, the chain. It is spoken of as pollution, as corruption, — in short, one would think that the Creator had imitated the cruelty of some Oriental despots who have been known to chain a festering corpse to a living body. Accordingly, the memoirs of these pious men are also mournful records of slow suicide, wrought by the persistent neglect of the most necessary and important laws of the bodily system ; and the body, outraged and down-trodden, has turned traitor to the soul, and played the adversary with fearful power. Who can tell the countless temptations to evil which flow in from a neglected, disordered, deranged nervous system, — temptations to anger, to irritability, to selfishness, to every kind of sin of appetite and passion ? No wonder that the poor soul longs for the hour of release from such a companion.

But that human body which God declares expressly was made to be the temple of the Holy Spirit, which

he considers worthy to be perpetuated by a resurrection and an immortal existence, cannot be intended
to be a clog and a hindrance to spiritual advancement. A perfect body, working in perfect tune and
time, would open glimpses of happiness to the soul
approaching the joys we hope for in heaven. It is
only through the images of things which our *bodily*
senses have taught us, that we can form any conception of that future bliss; and the more perfect these
senses, the more perfect our conceptions must be.

The conclusion of the whole matter, and the practical application of this sermon, is : — First, that all
men set themselves to form the idea of what perfect
health is, and resolve to realize it for themselves and
their children. Second, that with a view to this they
study the religion of the body, in such simple and
popular treatises as those of George Combe, Dr. Dio
Lewis, and others, and with simple and honest hearts
practise what they there learn. Third, that the training of the bodily system should form a regular part
of our common-school education, — every common
school being provided with a well-instructed teacher
of gymnastics; and the growth and development of
each pupil's body being as much noticed and marked
as is now the growth of his mind. The same course
should be continued and enlarged in colleges and
female seminaries, which should have professors of

hygiene appointed to give thorough instruction concerning the laws of health.

And when this is all done, we may hope that crooked spines, pimpled faces, sallow complexions, stooping shoulders, and all other signs indicating an undeveloped physical vitality, will, in the course of a few generations, disappear from the earth, and men will have bodies which will glorify God, their great Architect.

The soul of man has got as far as it can without the body. Religion herself stops and looks back, waiting for the body to overtake her. The soul's great enemy and hindrance can be made her best friend and most powerful help ; and it is high time that this era were begun. We old sinners, who have lived carelessly, and almost spent our day of grace, may not gain much of its good ; but the children, — shall there not be a more perfect day for them ? Shall there not come a day when the little child, whom Christ set forth to his disciples as the type of the greatest in the kingdom of heaven, shall be the type no less of our physical than our spiritual advancement, — when men and women shall arise, keeping through long and happy lives the simple, unperverted appetites, the joyous freshness of spirit, the keen delight in mere existence, the dreamless sleep and happy waking of early childhood ?

VII.

HOW SHALL WE ENTERTAIN OUR COMPANY?

"THE fact is," said Marianne, "we must have a party. Bob don't like to hear of it, but it must come. We are in debt to everybody : we have been invited everywhere, and never had anything like a party since we were married, and it won't do."

"For my part, I hate parties," said Bob. "They put your house all out of order, give all the women a sick-headache, and all the men an indigestion ; you never see anybody to any purpose ; the girls look bewitched, and the women answer you at cross-purposes, and call you by the name of your next-door neighbor, in their agitation of mind. We stay out beyond our usual bedtime, come home and find some baby crying, or child who has been sitting up till nobody knows when ; and the next morning, when I must be at my office by eight, and wife must attend to her children, we are sleepy and headachy. I protest against making overtures to entrap some hundred of my respectable married friends into this snare which has so often entangled me. If I had my way, I would never go to another party; and as to giving one — I suppose, since my empress has declared her intentions, that I shall be brought into doing it; but it shall be under protest."

"But, you see, we must keep up society," said Marianne.

"But I insist on it," said Bob, "it is n't keeping up society. What earthly thing do you learn about people by meeting them in a general crush, where all are coming, going, laughing, talking, and looking at each other? No person of common sense ever puts forth any idea he cares twopence about, under such circumstances; all that is exchanged is a certain set of commonplaces and platitudes which people keep for parties, just as they do their kid gloves and finery. Now there are our neighbors, the Browns. When they drop in of an evening, she knitting, and he with the last article in the paper, she really comes out with a great deal of fresh, lively, earnest, original talk. We have a good time, and I like her so much that it quite verges on loving; but see her in a party, when she manifests herself over five or six flounces of pink silk and a perfect egg-froth of tulle, her head adorned with a thicket of craped hair and roses, and it is plain at first view that *talking* with her is quite out of the question. What has been done to her head on the outside has evidently had some effect within, for she is no longer the Mrs. Brown you knew in her every-day dress, but Mrs. Brown in a party state of mind, and too distracted to think of anything in particular. She has a few words that she answers to everything you say, as, for example, 'O, very!' 'Certainly!' 'How extraordinary!' 'So happy to,' &c. The fact is, that she has come into a state in which any real communication with her mind and character must be suspended till the party is over and she is rested. Now I like society, which is the reason why I hate parties.

"But you see," said Marianne, "what are we to do? Everybody can't drop in to spend an evening with you. If it were not for these parties, there are quantities of your acquaintances whom you would never meet."

"And of what use is it to meet them? Do you really know them any better for meeting them got up in unusual dresses, and sitting down together when the only thing exchanged is the remark that it is hot or cold, or it rains, or it is dry, or any other patent surface-fact that answers the purpose of making believe you are talking when neither of you is saying a word?"

"Well, now, for my part," said Marianne, "I confess I *like* parties: they amuse me. I come home feeling kinder and better to people, just for the little I see of them when they are all dressed up and in good humor with themselves. To be sure we don't say anything very profound, — I don't think the most of us have anything very profound to say ; but I ask Mrs. Brown where she buys her lace, and she tells me how she washes it, and somebody else tells me about her baby, and promises me a new sack-pattern. Then I like to see the pretty, nice young girls flirting with the nice young men ; and I like to be dressed up a little myself, even if my finery is all old and many times made over. It does me good to be rubbed up and brightened."

"Like old silver," said Bob.

"Yes, like old silver, precisely ; and even if I do come home tired, it does my mind good to have that change of scene and faces. You men do not know what it is to be tied to house and nursery all day, and what a perfect weariness and lassitude it often brings on us women. For my part, I think parties are a beneficial institution of society, and that it is worth a good deal of fatigue and trouble to get one up."

"Then there's the expense," said Bob. "What earthly need is there of a grand regale of oysters, chicken-salad, ice-creams, coffee, and champagne, between eleven and twelve o'clock at night, when no one of us would ever think of wanting or taking any

8

such articles upon our stomachs in our own homes? If we were all of us in the habit of having a regular repast at that hour, it might be well enough to enjoy one with our neighbor; but the party fare is generally just so much in addition to the honest three meals which we have eaten during the day. Now, to spend from fifty to one, two, or three hundred dollars in giving all our friends an indigestion from a midnight meal seems to me a very poor investment. Yet if we once begin to give the party, we must have everything that is given at the other parties, or wherefore do we live? And caterers and waiters rack their brains to devise new forms of expense and extravagance; and when the bill comes in, one is sure to feel that one is paying a great deal of money for a great deal of nonsense. It is, in fact, worse than nonsense, because our dear friends are, in half the cases, not only no better, but a great deal worse, for what they have eaten."

"But there is this advantage to society," said Rudolph, — "it helps us young physicians. What would the physicians do if parties were abolished? Take all the colds that are caught by our fair friends with low necks and short sleeves, all the troubles from dancing in tight dresses and inhaling bad air, and all the headaches and indigestions from the *mélange* of lobster-salad, two or three kinds of ice-cream, cake, and coffee on delicate stomachs, and our profession gets a degree of encouragement that is worthy to be thought of."

"But the question arises," said my wife, "whether there are not ways of promoting social feeling less expensive, more simple and natural and rational. I am inclined to think that there are."

"Yes," said Theophilus Thoro ; "for large parties are not, as a general thing, given with any wish or intention of really improving our acquaintance with our neighbors. In many cases they are openly and avowedly a general tribute paid at intervals to society, for and in consideration of which you are to sit with closed blinds and doors and be let alone for the rest of the year. Mrs. Bogus, for instance, lives to keep her house in order, her closets locked, her silver counted and in the safe, and her china-closet in un-disturbed order. Her 'best things' are put away with such admirable precision, in so many wrappings and foldings, and secured with so many a twist and twine, that to get them out is one of the seven labors of Hercules, not to be lightly or unadvisedly taken in hand, but reverently, discreetly, and once for all, in an annual or biennial party. Then says Mrs. Bogus, 'For Heaven's sake, let's have every creature we can think of, and have 'em all over with at once. For pity's sake, let's have no driblets left that we shall have to be inviting to dinner or to tea. No matter whether they can come or not, — only send them the invitation, and our part is done ; and, thank Heaven ! we shall be free for a year.'"

"Yes," said my wife; "a great stand - up party bears just the same relation towards the offer of real hospitality and good-will as Miss Sally Brass's offer of meat to the little hungry Marchioness, when, with a bit uplifted on the end of a fork, she addressed her, 'Will you have this piece of meat ? No ? Well, then, remember and don't say you have n't had meat *offered* to you !' You are invited to a general jam, at the risk of your life and health ; and if you refuse, don't say you have n't had hospitality offered to you. All our debts are wiped out and our slate clean ; now we will have our own closed doors, no company and no trouble, and our best china shall repose undisturbed on its shelves. Mrs. Bogus says she never could exist in the way that Mrs. Easygo does, with a constant drip of company, — two or three to breakfast one day, half a dozen to dinner the next, and little evening gatherings once or twice a week. It must keep her house in confusion all the time ; yet, for real social feeling, real exchange of thought and opinion, there is more of it in one half-hour at Mrs. Easygo's than in a dozen of Mrs. Bogus's great parties.

"The fact is, that Mrs. Easygo really does like the society of human beings. She is genuinely and heartily social ; and, in consequence, though she has very limited means, and no money to spend in giving great entertainments, her domestic establishment is a sort of social exchange, where more friendships are formed, more real acquaintance made, and more agreeable hours spent, than in any other place that can be named. She never has large parties, — great general pay-days of social debts, — but small, well-chosen circles of people, selected so thoughtfully, with a view to the pleasure which congenial persons give each other, as to make the invitation an act of real personal kindness. She always manages to have something for the entertainment of her friends, so that they are not reduced to the simple alternatives of gaping at each other's dresses and eating lobster-salad and ice-cream. There is either some choice music, or a reading of fine poetry, or a well-acted charade, or a portfolio of photographs and pictures, to enliven the hour and start conversation ; and as the people are skilfully chosen with reference to each other, as there is no hurry or heat or confusion, conversation, in its best sense, can bubble up, fresh, genuine, clear, and sparkling as a woodland spring, and one goes away really rested and refreshed. The slight entertainment provided is just enough to enable you to eat salt together in Arab fashion, — not enough to form the leading feature of the evening. A cup of tea and a basket of cake, or a salver of ices, silently passed **at** quiet intervals, do not interrupt conversation or over-load the stomach."

" The fact is," said I, " that the art of society among us Anglo-Saxons is yet in its ruder stages. We are not, as a race, social and confiding, like the French and Italians and Germans. We have a word for home, and our home is often a moated grange, an island, a castle with its drawbridge up, cutting us off from all but our own home-circle. In France and Germany and Italy there are the boulevards and pub-lic gardens, where people do their family living in common. Mr. A. is breakfasting under one tree, with wife and children around, and Mr. B. is breakfasting under another tree, hard by ; and messages, nods, and smiles pass backward and forward. Families see each other daily in these public resorts, and exchange mutual offices of good-will. Perhaps from these cus-toms of society come that naïve simplicity and *aban-don* which one remarks in the Continental, in opposi-tion to the Anglo-Saxon, habits of conversation. A Frenchman or an Italian will talk to you of his feel-ings and plans and prospects with an unreserve that is perfectly unaccountable to you, who have always felt that such things must be kept for the very inner-most circle of home privacy. But the Frenchman or Italian has from a child been brought up to pass his family life in places of public resort, in constant contact and intercommunion with other families ; and the social and conversational instinct has thus been daily strengthened. Hence the reunions of these people have been characterized by a sprightliness and vigor and spirit that the Anglo-Saxon has in vain attempted to seize and reproduce. English and American *conversazioni* have very generally proved a failure, from the rooted, frozen habit of reticence and reserve which grows with our growth and strengthens with our strength. The fact is, that the Anglo-Saxon race as a race does not enjoy talking, and, except in rare instances, does not talk well. A daily convocation of people, without refreshments or any extraneous object but the simple pleasure of seeing and talking with each other, is a thing that can scarcely be understood in English or American society. Social entertainment presupposes in the Anglo-Saxon mind *something to eat*, and not only something, but a great deal. Enormous dinners or great suppers constitute the entertainment. Nobody seems to have formed the idea that the talking — the simple exchange of the social feelings — *is*, of itself, the entertainment, and that *being together* is the pleasure.

" Madame Recamier for years had a circle of friends who met every afternoon in her *salon* from four to six o'clock, for the simple and sole pleasure of talking with each other. The very first wits and men of letters and statesmen and *savans* were enrolled in it, and each brought to the entertainment some choice *morceau* which he had laid aside from his own particular field to add to the feast. The daily intimacy gave each one such perfect insight into all the others' habits of thought, tastes, and preferences, that the conversation was like the celebrated music of the *Conservatoire* in Paris, a concert of perfectly chorded instruments taught by long habit of harmonious intercourse to keep exact time and tune together.

"*Real* conversation presupposes intimate acquaintance. People must see each other often enough to wear off the rough bark and outside rind of commonplaces and conventionalities in which their real ideas are enwrapped, and give forth without reserve their innermost and best feelings. Now what is called a large party is the first and rudest form of social intercourse. The most we can say of it is, that it is better than nothing. Men and women are crowded together like cattle in a pen. They look at each other, they jostle each other, exchange a few common bleatings, and eat together; and so the performance terminates. One may be crushed evening after evening against men or women, and learn very little about them. You may decide that a lady is good-tempered, when any amount of trampling on the skirt of her new silk dress brings no cloud to her brow. But *is* it good temper, or only wanton carelessness, which cares nothing for waste? You can see that a man is not a gentleman who squares his back to ladies at the supper-table, and devours boned turkey and *paté de fois gras*, while they vainly reach over and around him for something, and that another is a gentleman so far as to prefer the care of his weaker neighbors to the immediate indulgence of his own appetites; but further than this you learn little. Sometimes, it is true, in some secluded corner, two people of fine nervous system, undisturbed by the general confusion, may have a sociable half-hour, and really part feeling that they like each other better, and know more of each other than before. Yet these general gatherings have, after all, their value. They are not so good as something better would be, but they cannot be wholly dispensed with. It is far better that Mrs. Bogus should give an annual party, when she takes down all her bedsteads and throws open her whole house, than that she should never see her friends and neighbors inside her doors at all. She may feel that she has neither the taste nor the talent for constant small reunions. Such things, she may feel, require a social tact which she has not. She would be utterly at a loss how to conduct them. Each one would cost her as much anxiety and thought as her annual gathering, and prove

8*   L

a failure after all; whereas the annual demonstration can be put wholly into the hands of the caterer, who comes in force, with flowers, silver, china, servants, and, taking the house into his own hands, gives her entertainment for her, leaving to her no responsibility but the payment of the bills; and if Mr. Bogus does not quarrel with them, we know no reason why any one else should; and I think Mrs. Bogus merits well of the republic, for doing what she can do towards the hospitalities of the season. I'm sure I never cursed her in my heart, even when her strong coffee has held mine eyes open till morning, and her superlative lobster-salads have given me the very darkest views of human life that ever dyspepsia and east wind could engender. Mrs. Bogus is the Eve who offers the apple; but, after all, I am the foolish Adam who take and eat what I know is going to hurt me, and I am too gallant to visit my sins on the head of my too obliging tempter. In country places in particular, where little is going on and life is apt to stagnate, a good, large, generous party, which brings the whole neighborhood into one house to have a jolly time, to eat, drink, and be merry, is really quite a work of love and mercy. People see one another in their best clothes, and that is something; the elders exchange all manner of simple pleasantries and civilities, and talk over their domestic affairs, while the young people flirt, in that wholesome manner which is one of the safest of youthful follies. A country party, in fact, may be set down as a work of benevolence, and the money expended thereon fairly charged to the account of the great cause of peace and good-will on earth."

" But don't you think," said my wife, " that, if the charge of providing the entertainment were less laborious, these gatherings could be more frequent ? You see, if a woman feels that she must have five kinds of cake, and six kinds of preserves, and even ice-cream and jellies in a region where no confectioner comes in to abbreviate her labors, she will sit with closed doors, and do nothing towards the general exchange of life, because she cannot do as much as Mrs. Smith or Mrs. Parsons. If the idea of meeting together had some other focal point than eating, I think there would be more social feeling. It might be a musical reunion, where the various young people of a circle agreed to furnish each a song or an instrumental performance. It might be an impromptu charade party, bringing out something of that taste in arrangement of costume, and capacity for dramatic effect, of which there is more latent in society than we think. It might be the reading of articles in prose and poetry furnished to a common paper or portfolio, which would awaken an abundance of interest and specula-

tion on the authorship, or it might be dramatic readings and recitations. Any or all of these pastimes
might make an evening so entertaining that a simple
cup of tea and a plate of cake or biscuit would be all
the refreshment needed."

"We may with advantage steal a leaf now and
then from some foreign book," said I. "In France
and Italy, families have their peculiar days set apart
for the reception of friends at their own houses.
The whole house is put upon a footing of hospitality
and invitation, and the whole mind is given to receiving the various friends. In the evening the *salon* is
filled. The guests, coming from week to week, for
years, become in time friends ; the resort has the
charm of a home circle ; there are certain faces that
you are always sure to meet there. A lady once said
to me of a certain gentleman and lady whom she
missed from her circle, 'They have been at our house
every Wednesday evening for twenty years.' It seems
to me that this frequency of meeting is the great
secret of agreeable society. One sees, in our American life, abundance of people who are everything that
is charming and cultivated, but one never sees enough
of them. One meets them at some quiet reunion,
passes a delightful hour, thinks how charming they
are, and wishes one could see more of them. But the
pleasant meeting is like the encounter of two ships in

mid-ocean away we sail, each on his respective course, to see each other no more till the pleasant remembrance has died away. Yet were there some quiet, home-like resort where we might turn in to renew from time to time the pleasant intercourse, to continue the last conversation, and to compare anew our readings and our experiences, the pleasant hour of liking would ripen into a warm friendship.

" But in order that this may be made possible and practicable, the utmost simplicity of entertainment must prevail. In a French *salon*, all is, to the last degree, informal. The *bouilloire*, the French tea-kettle, is often tended by one of the gentlemen, who aids his fair neighbors in the mysteries of tea-making. One nymph is always to be found at the table dispensing tea and talk ; and a basket of simple biscuit and cakes, offered by another, is all the further repast. The teacups and cake-basket are a real addition to the scene, because they cause a little lively social bustle, a little chatter and motion, — always of advantage in breaking up stiffness, and giving occasion for those graceful, airy nothings that answer so good a purpose in facilitating acquaintance.

" Nothing can be more charming than the description which Edmond About gives, in his novel of 'Tolla,' of the reception evenings of an old noble Roman family, — the spirit of repose and quietude through all the apartments, — the ease of coming and going, — the perfect homelike spirit in which the guests settle themselves to any employment of the hour that best suits them, — some to lively chat, some to dreamy, silent lounging, some to a game, others, in a distant apartment, to music, and others still to a promenade along the terraces.

"One is often in a state of mind and nerves which indisposes for the effort of active conversation; one wishes to rest, to observe, to be amused without an effort; and a mansion which opens wide its hospitable arms, and offers itself to you as a sort of home, where you may rest, and do just as the humor suits you, is a perfect godsend at such times. You are at home there, your ways are understood, you can do as you please, — come early or late, be brilliant or dull, — you are always welcome. If you can do nothing for the social whole to-night, it matters not. There are many more nights to come in the future, and you are entertained on trust, without a challenge.

"I have one friend, — a man of genius, subject to the ebbs and flows of animal spirits which attend that organization. Of general society he has a nervous horror. A regular dinner or evening party is to him a terror, an impossibility; but there is a quiet parlor where stands a much-worn old sofa, and it is his delight to enter without knocking, and be found lying with half-shut eyes on this friendly couch, while the family life goes on around him without a question. Nobody is to mind him, to tease him with inquiries or salutations. If he will, he breaks into the stream of conversation, and sometimes, rousing up from one of these dreamy trances, finds himself, ere he or they know how, in the mood for free and friendly talk. People often wonder, ' How do you catch So-and-so? He is so shy! I have invited and invited, and he never comes.' We never invite, and he comes. We take no note of his coming or his going ; we do not startle his entrance with acclamation, nor clog his departure with expostulation ; it is fully understood that with us he shall do just as he chooses ; and so he chooses to do much that we like.

" The sum of this whole doctrine of society is, that we are to try the value of all modes and forms of social entertainment by their effect in producing real acquaintance and real friendship and good-will. The first and rudest form of seeking this is by a great promiscuous party, which simply effects this, — that people at least see each other on the outside, and eat together. Next come all those various forms of reunion in which the entertainment consists of some-thing higher than staring and eating, — some exercise of the faculties of the guests in music, acting, recita-tion, reading, etc. ; and these are a great advance, because they show people what is in them, and thus lay a foundation for a more intelligent appreciation and acquaintance. These are the best substitute for the expense, show, and trouble of large parties. They are in their nature more refining and intellectual. It is astonishing, when people really put together, in some one club or association, all the different talents for pleasing possessed by different persons, how clever a circle may be gathered, — in the least promising neighborhood. A club of ladies in one of our cities has had quite a brilliant success. It is held every fortnight at the house of the members, according to alphabetical sequence. The lady who receives has charge of arranging what the entertainment shall be, — whether charade, tableau, reading, recitation, or music ; and the interest is much increased by the individual taste shown in the choice of the diversion and the variety which thence follows.

"In the summer time, in the country, open-air reunions are charming forms of social entertainment. Croquet parties, which bring young people together by daylight for a healthy exercise, and end with a moderate share of the evening, are a very desirable amusement. What are called 'lawn teas' are finding great favor in England and some parts of our country. They are simply an early tea enjoyed in a sort of picnic style in the grounds about the house. Such an entertainment enables one to receive a great many at a time, without crowding, and, being in its very idea rustic and informal, can be arranged with very little expense or trouble. With the addition of lanterns in the trees and a little music, this entertainment may be carried on far into the evening with a very pretty effect.

" As to dancing, I have this much to say of it. Either our houses must be all built over and made larger, or female crinolines must be made smaller, or dancing must continue as it now is, the most absurd and ungraceful of all attempts at amusement. The effort to execute round dances in the limits of modern houses, in the prevailing style of dress, can only lead to developments more startling than agreeable. Dancing in the open air, on the shaven green of lawns, is a pretty and graceful exercise, and there only can full sweep be allowed for the present feminine toilet.

" The English breakfast is an institution growing in favor here, and rightfully, too ; for a party of fresh, good-natured, well-dressed people, assembled at breakfast on a summer morning, is as nearly perfect a form of reunion as can be devised. All are in full strength from their night's rest; the hour is fresh and lovely, and they are in condition to give each other the very cream of their thoughts, the first keen sparkle of the uncorked nervous system. The only drawback is, that, in our busy American life, the most desirable gentlemen often cannot spare their morning hours. Breakfast parties presuppose a condition of leisure; but when they can be compassed, they are perhaps the most perfectly enjoyable of entertainments."

"Well," said Marianne, "I begin to waver about my party. I don't know, after all, but the desire of paying off social debts prompted the idea; perhaps we might try some of the agreeable things suggested. But, dear me! there's the baby. We'll finish the talk some other time."

VIII.

HOW SHALL WE BE AMUSED?

"ONE, two, three, four, — this makes the fifth accident on the Fourth of July, in the two papers I have just read," said Jenny.

"A very moderate allowance," said Theophilus Thoro, "if you consider the Fourth as a great national saturnalia, in which every boy in the land has the privilege of doing whatever is right in his own eyes."

"The poor boys!" said Mrs. Crowfield. "All the troubles of the world are laid at their door."

"Well," said Jenny, "they did burn the city of Portland, it appears. The fire arose from fire-crackers, thrown by boys among the shavings of a carpenter's shop, — so says the paper."

"And," said Rudolph, "we surgeons expect a harvest of business from the Fourth, as surely as from a battle. Certain to be woundings, fractures, possibly amputations, following the proceedings of our glorious festival."

"Why cannot we Americans learn to amuse ourselves peaceably like other nations?" said Bob Stephens. "In France and Italy, the greatest national festivals pass off without fatal accident, or danger to any one. The fact is, in our country we have not learned *how to be amused*. Amusement has been made of so small account in our philosophy of life, that we are raw and unpractised in being amused. Our diversions, compared with those of the politer nations of Europe, are coarse and savage, — and consist mainly in making disagreeable noises and disturbing the peace of the community by rude uproar. The only idea an American boy associates with the Fourth of July is that of gunpowder in some form, and a wild liberty to fire off pistols in all miscellaneous directions, and to throw fire-crackers under the heels of horses, and into crowds of women and children, for the fun of seeing the stir and commotion thus produced. Now take a young Parisian boy and give him a fête, and he conducts himself with greater gentleness and good breeding, because he is part of a community in which the art of amusement has been refined and perfected, so that he has a thousand resources beyond the very obvious one of making a great banging and disturbance.

"Yes," continued Bob Stephens, "the fact is, that our grim old Puritan fathers set their feet down resolutely on all forms of amusement; they would have stopped the lambs from wagging their tails, and shot the birds for singing, if they could have had their way; and in consequence of it, what a barren, cold, flowerless life is our New England existence! Life is all, as Mantalini said, one 'demd horrid grind.' 'Nothing here but working and going to church,' said the German emigrants, — and they were about right. A French traveller, in the year 1837, says that attending the Thursday-evening lectures and church prayer-meetings was the only recreation of the young people of Boston; and we can remember the time when this really was no exaggeration. Think of that, with all the seriousness of our Boston east winds to give it force, and fancy the provision for amusement in our society! The consequence is, that boys who have the longing for amusement strongest within them, and plenty of combativeness to back it, are the standing terror of good society, and our Fourth of July is a day of fear to all invalids and persons of delicate nervous organization, and of real, appreciable danger of life and limb to every one."

"Well, Robert," said my wife, "though I agree with you as to the actual state of society in this respect, I must enter my protest against your slur on the memory of our Pilgrim fathers."

"Yes," said Theophilus Thoro, "the New-Englanders are the only people, I believe, who take delight in vilifying their ancestry. Every young hopeful in our day makes a target of his grandfather's grave-stone, and fires away, with great self-applause. People in general seem to like to show that they are well-born, and come of good stock; but the young New-Englanders, many of them, appear to take pleasure in insisting that they came of a race of narrow-minded, persecuting bigots.

"It is true, that our Puritan fathers saw not every-thing. They made a state where there were no amusements, but where people could go to bed and leave their house doors wide open all night, without a shadow of fear or danger, as was for years the custom in all our country villages. The fact is, that the simple early New England life, before we began to import foreigners, realized a state of society in whose possibility Europe would scarcely believe. If our fathers had few amusements, they needed few. Life was too really and solidly comfortable and happy to need much amusement.

"Look over the countries where people are most sedulously amused by their rulers and governors. Are they not the countries where the people are most oppressed, most unhappy in their circumstances, and therefore in greatest need of amusement? It is the slave who dances and sings, and why? Because be

owns nothing, and *can* own nothing, and may as well
dance and forget the fact. But give the slave a farm
of his own, a wife of his own, and children of his own,
with a school-house and a vote, and ten to one he
dances no more. He needs no *amusement*, because
he is *happy*.

"The legislators of Europe wished nothing more
than to bring up a people who would be content with
amusements, and not ask after their rights or think
too closely how they were governed. 'Gild the dome
of the Invalides,' was Napoleon's scornful prescrip-
tion, when he heard the Parisian population were dis-
contented. They gilded it, and the people forgot to
talk about anything else. They were a childish race,
educated from the cradle on spectacle and show, and
by the sight of their eyes could they be governed.
The people of Boston, in 1776, could not have been
managed in this way, chiefly because they were
brought up in the strict schools of the fathers."

"But don't you think," said Jenny, "that something
might be added and amended in the state of society
our fathers established here in New England? Without becoming frivolous, there might be more attention
paid to rational amusement."

"Certainly," said my wife, "the State and the
Church both might take a lesson from the providence
of foreign governments, and make liberty, to say the

least, as attractive as despotism. It is a very unwise mother that does not provide her children with playthings."

"And yet," said Bob, "the only thing that the Church has yet done is to forbid and to frown. We have abundance of tracts against dancing, whist-playing, ninepins, billiards, operas, theatres, — in short, anything that young people would be apt to like. The General Assembly of the Presbyterian Church refused to testify against slavery, because of political diffidence, but made up for it by ordering a more stringent crusade against dancing. The theatre and opera grow up and exist among us like plants on the windy side of a hill, blown all awry by a constant blast of conscientious rebuke. There is really no amusement young people are fond of, which they do not pursue, in a sort of defiance of the frown of the peculiarly religious world. With all the telling of what the young shall *not* do, there has been very little telling what they shall do.

"The whole department of amusements — certainly one of the most important in education — has been by the Church made a sort of outlaws' ground, to be taken possession of and held by all sorts of spiritual ragamuffins ; and then the faults and short-comings resulting from this arrangement have been held up and insisted on as reasons why no Christian should ever venture into it.

"If the Church would set herself to amuse her young folks, instead of discussing doctrines and metaphysical hair-splitting, she would prove herself a true mother, and not a hard-visaged step-dame. Let her keep this department, so powerful and so difficult to manage, in what are morally the strongest hands, instead of giving it up to the weakest.

"I think, if the different churches of a city, for example, would rent a building where there should be a billiard-table, one or two ninepin-alleys, a reading-room, a garden and grounds for ball-playing or innocent lounging, that they would do more to keep their young people from the ways of sin than a Sunday school could. Nay, more: I would go further. I would have a portion of the building fitted up with scenery and a stage, for the getting up of tableaux or dramatic performances, and thus give scope for the exercise of that histrionic talent of which there is so much lying unemployed in society.

"Young people do not like amusements any better for the wickedness connected with them. The spectacle of a sweet little child singing hymns, and repeating prayers, of a pious old Uncle Tom dying for his religion, has filled theatres night after night, and proved that there really is no need of indecent or improper plays to draw full houses.

"The things that draw young people to places of

9   M

amusement are not at first gross things. Take the most notorious public place in Paris, — the Jardin Mabille, for instance, — and the things which give it its first charm are all innocent and artistic. Exquisite beds of lilies, roses, gillyflowers, lighted with jets of gas so artfully as to make every flower translucent as a gem ; fountains where the gas-light streams out from behind misty wreaths of falling water and calla-blossoms ; sofas of velvet turf, canopied with fragrant honeysuckle ; dim bowers overarched with lilacs and roses ; a dancing ground under trees whose branches bend with a fruitage of many-colored lamps ; enchanting music and graceful motion ; in all these there is not only no sin, but they are really beautiful and desirable ; and if they were only used on the side and in the service of virtue and religion, if they were contrived and kept up by the guardians and instructors of youth, instead of by those whose interest it is to demoralize and destroy, young people would have no temptation to stray into the haunts of vice.

"In Prussia, under the reign of Frederick William II., when one good, hard-handed man governed the whole country like a strict schoolmaster, the public amusements for the people were made such as to present a model for all states. The theatres were strictly supervised, and actors obliged to conform to the rules of decorum and morality. The plays and performances were under the immediate supervision of men of grave morals, who allowed nothing corrupting to appear; and the effect of this administration and restraint is to be seen in Berlin even to this day. The public gardens are full of charming little resorts, where, every afternoon, for a very moderate sum, one can have either a concert of good music, or a very fair dramatic or operatic performance. Here whole families may be seen enjoying together a wholesome and refreshing entertainment, — the mother and aunts with their knitting, the baby, the children of all ages, and the father, — their faces radiant with that mild German light of contentment and good-will which one feels to be characteristic of the nation. When I saw these things, and thought of our own outcast, unprovided boys and young men, haunting the streets and alleys of cities, in places far from the companionship of mothers and sisters, I felt as if it would be better for a nation to be brought up by a good strict schoolmaster king than to try to be a republic."

"Yes," said I, "but the difficulty is to *get* the good schoolmaster king. For one good shepherd, there are twenty who use the sheep only for their flesh and their wool. Republics can do all that kings can, — witness our late army and Sanitary Commission. Once fix the idea thoroughly in the public mind that there ought to be as regular and careful provision for public amusement as there is for going to church and Sunday school, and it will be done.   Central Park in New York is a beginning in the right direction, and Brooklyn is following the example of her sister city. There is, moreover, an indication of the proper spirit in the increased efforts that are made to beautify Sunday-school rooms, and make them interesting, and to have Sunday-school fêtes and picnics, — the most harmless and commendable way of celebrating the Fourth of July.   Why should saloons and bar-rooms be made attractive by fine paintings, choice music, flowers, and fountains, and Sunday-school rooms be four bare walls?   There are churches whose broad aisles represent ten and twenty millions of dollars, and whose sons and daughters are daily drawn to circuses, operas, theatres, because they have tastes and feelings, in themselves perfectly laudable and innocent, for the gratification of which no provision is made in any other place."

"I know one church," said Rudolph, "whose Sunday-school room is as beautifully adorned as any haunt of sin.   There is a fountain in the centre, which plays into a basin surrounded with shells and flowers; it has a small organ to lead the children's voices, and the walls are hung with oil-paintings and engravings from the best masters.   The festivals of the Sabbath school, which are from time to time held in this place, educate the taste of the children, as well as amuse them; and, above all, they have through life the advantage of associating with their early religious education all those ideas of taste, elegance, and artistic culture which too often come through polluted channels.

"When the *amusement* of the young shall become the care of the experienced and the wise, and the floods of wealth that are now rolling over and over, in silent investments, shall be put into the form of innocent and refined pleasures for the children and youth of the state, our national festivals may become days to be desired, and not dreaded.

"On the Fourth of July, our city fathers do in a certain dim wise perceive that the public owes some attempt at amusement to its children, and they vote large sums, principally expended in bell-ringing, cannons, and fireworks. The side-walks are witness to the number who fall victims to the temptations held out by grog-shops and saloons; and the papers, for weeks after, are crowded with accounts of accidents. Now, a yearly sum expended to keep up, and keep pure, places of amusement which hold out no temptation to vice, but which excel all vicious places in real beauty and attractiveness, would greatly lessen the sum needed to be expended on any one particular day, and would refine and prepare our people to keep holidays and festivals appropriately."

"For my part," said Mrs. Crowfield, "I am grieved at the opprobrium which falls on the race of *boys.* Why should the most critical era in the life of those who are to be men, and to *govern* society, be passed in a sort of outlawry, — a rude warfare with all existing institutions? The years between ten and twenty are full of the nervous excitability which marks the growth and maturing of the manly nature. The boy feels wild impulses, which ought to be vented in legitimate and healthful exercise. He wants to run, shout, wrestle, ride, row, skate ; and all these together are often not sufficient to relieve the need he feels of throwing off the excitability that burns within.

"For the wants of this period what safe provision is made by the Church, or by the State, or any of the boy's lawful educators? In all the Prussian schools amusements are as much a part of the regular school-system as grammar or geography. The teacher is with the boys on the play-ground, and plays as heartily as any of them. The boy has his physical wants anticipated. He is not left to fight his way, blindly stumbling against society, but goes forward in a safe path, which his elders and betters have marked out for him.

"In our country, the boy's career is often a series of skirmishes with society. He wants to skate, and contrives ingeniously to dam the course of a brook

and flood a meadow which makes a splendid skating-
ground.   Great is the joy for a season, and great the
skating.   But the water floods the neighboring cel-
lars.   The boys are cursed through all the moods and
tenses, — boys are such a plague !   The dam is torn
down with emphasis and execration.   The boys, however, lie in wait some cold night, between twelve and
one, and build it up again ; and thus goes on the battle.   The boys care not whose cellar they flood, because nobody cares for their amusement.   They understand themselves to be outlaws, and take an out-
law's advantage.

"Again, the boys have their sleds ; and sliding
down hill is splendid fun.   But they trip up some
grave citizen, who sprains his shoulder.   What is the
result ?   Not the provision of a safe, good place,
where boys *may* slide down hill without danger to
any one, but an edict forbidding all sliding, under
penalty of fine.

" Boys want to swim : it is best they should swim ;
and if city fathers, foreseeing and caring for this want,
should think it worth while to mark off some good
place, and have it under such police surveillance as
to enforce decency of language and demeanor, they
would prevent a great deal that now is disagreeable in
the unguided efforts of boys to enjoy this luxury.

" It would be *cheaper* in the end, even if one had to

build sliding-piles, as they do in Russia, or to build skating-rinks, as they do in Montreal, — it would be cheaper for every city, town, and village to provide legitimate amusement for boys, under proper superintendence, than to leave them, as they are now left, to fight their way against society.

" In the boys' academies of our country, what provision is made for amusement ? There are stringent rules, and any number of them, to prevent boys making any noise that may disturb the neighbors ; and generally the teacher thinks that, if he keeps the boys *still*, and sees that they get their lessons, his duty is done. But a hundred boys ought not to be kept still. There ought to be noise and motion among them, in order that they may healthily survive the great changes which Nature is working within them. If they become silent, averse to movement, fond of indoor lounging and warm rooms, they are going in far worse ways than any amount of outward lawlessness could bring them to.

" Smoking and yellow-covered novels are worse than any amount of hullabaloo ; and the quietest boy is often a poor, ignorant victim, whose life is being drained out of him before it is well begun. If mothers could only see the *series of books* that are sold behind counters to boarding-school boys, whom nobody warns and nobody cares for, — if they could see the

poison, going from pillow to pillow, in books pretending to make clear the great, sacred mysteries of our
nature, but trailing them over with the filth of utter
corruption! These horrible works are the inward and
secret channel of hell, into which a boy is thrust by
the pressure of strict outward rules, forbidding that
physical and out-of-door exercise and motion to
which he ought rather to be encouraged, and even
driven.

"It is melancholy to see that, while parents, teachers, and churches make no provision for boys in the
way of amusement, the world, the flesh, and the Devil
are incessantly busy and active in giving it to them.
There are ninepin-alleys, with cigars and a bar.
There are billiard-saloons, with a bar, and, alas!
with the occasional company of girls who are still
beautiful, but who have lost the innocence of womanhood, while yet retaining many of its charms. There
are theatres, with a bar, and with the society of lost
women. The boy comes to one and all of these places, seeking only what is natural and proper he should
have, — what should be given him under the eye and
by the care of the Church, the school. He comes for
exercise and amusement, — he gets these, and a ticket
to destruction besides, — and whose fault is it?"

"These are the aspects of public life," said I,
"which make me feel that we never shall have a per-

9*

fect state till women vote and bear rule equally with men. State housekeeping has been, hitherto, like what any housekeeping would be, conducted by the voice and knowledge of man alone.

" If women had an equal voice in the management of our public money, I have faith to believe that thousands which are now wasted in mere political charlatanism would go to provide for the rearing of the children of the state, male and female. My wife has spoken for the boys ; I speak for the girls also. What is provided for their physical development and amusement? Hot, gas-lighted theatric and operatic performances, beginning at eight, and ending at midnight ; hot, crowded parties and balls ; dancing with dresses tightly laced over the laboring lungs, — these are almost the whole story. I bless the advent of croquet and skating. And yet the latter exercise, pursued as it generally is, is a most terrible exposure. There is no kindly parental provision for the poor, thoughtless, delicate young creature, — not even the shelter of a dressing-room with a fire, at which she may warm her numb fingers and put on her skates when she arrives on the ground, and to which she may retreat in inter·vals of fatigue ; so she catches cold, and perhaps sows the seed which with air-tight stoves and other appli·ances of hot-house culture may ripen into consump·tion.

" What provision is there for the amusement of all the shop girls, seamstresses, factory girls, that crowd our cities? What for the thousands of young clerks and operatives? Not long since, in a respectable old town in New England, the body of a beautiful girl was drawn from the river in which she had drowned herself, — a young girl only fifteen, who came to the city, far from home and parents, and fell a victim to the temptation which brought her to shame and desperation. Many thus fall every year who are never counted. They fall into the ranks of those whom the world abandons as irreclaimable.

" Let those who have homes and every appliance to make life pass agreeably, and who yet yawn over an unoccupied evening, fancy a lively young girl all day cooped up at sewing in a close, ill-ventilated room. Evening comes, and she has three times the desire for amusement and three times the need of it that her fashionable sister has. And where can she go? To the theatre, perhaps, with some young man as thoughtless as herself, and more depraved ; then to the bar for a glass of wine, and another ; and then, with a head swimming and turning, who shall say where else she may be led? Past midnight and no one to look after her, — and one night ruins her utterly and for life, and she as yet only a child !

" John Newton had a very wise saying : ' Here is a

man trying to fill a bushel with chaff. Now if I fill it with wheat first, it is better than to fight him.' This apothegm contains in it the whole of what I would say on the subject of amusements."

IX.

DRESS, OR WHO MAKES THE FASHIONS.

THE door of my study being open, I heard in the distant parlor a sort of flutter of silken wings, and chatter of bird-like voices, which told me that a covey of Jennie's pretty young street birds had just alighted there. I could not forbear a peep at the rosy faces that glanced out under pheasants' tails, doves' wings, and nodding humming-birds, and made one or two errands in that direction only that I might gratify my eyes with a look at them.

Your nice young girl, of good family and good breeding, is always a pretty object, and, for my part, I regularly lose my heart (in a sort of figurative way) to every fresh, charming creature that trips across my path. All their mysterious rattle-traps and whirligigs, — their curls and networks and crimples and rimples and crisping-pins, — their little absurdities, if you will, — have to me a sort of charm, like the tricks and stammerings of a curly-headed child. I should have made a very poor censor if I had been put in Cato's place : the witches would have thrown all my wisdom into some private chip-basket of their own, and walked off with it in triumph.   Never a girl bows to me that I do not see in her eye a twinkle of confidence that she could, if she chose, make an old fool of me.   I surrender at discretion on first sight.

Jennie's friends are nice girls, — the flowers of good, staid, sensible families, — not heathen blossoms nursed in the hot-bed heat of wild, high-flying, fashionable society.   They have been duly and truly taught and brought up, by good mothers and painstaking aunties, to understand in their infancy that handsome is that handsome does ; that little girls must not be vain of their pretty red shoes and nice curls, and must remember that it is better to be good than to be handsome ; with all other wholesome truisms of the kind.   They have been to school, and had their minds improved in all modern ways, — have calculated eclipses, and read Virgil, Schiller, and La Fontaine, and understand all about the geological strata, and the different systems of metaphysics, — so that a person reading the list of their acquirements might be a little appalled at the prospect of entering into conversation with them. For all these reasons I listened quite indulgently to the animated conversation that was going on about — Well !

What *do* girls generally talk about, when a knot of them get together? Not, I believe, about the sources of the Nile, or the precession of the equinoxes, or the nature of the human understanding, or Dante, or Shakespeare, or Milton, although they have learned all about them in school; but upon a theme much nearer and dearer, — the one all-pervading feminine topic ever since Eve started the first toilet of fig-leaves; and as I caught now and then a phrase of their chatter, I jotted it down in pure amusement, giving to each charming speaker the name of the bird under whose colors she was sailing.

"For my part," said little Humming-Bird, "I'm quite worn out with sewing; the fashions are all *so* different from what they were last year, that everything has to be made over."

"Is n't it dreadful!" said Pheasant. "There's my new mauve silk dress! it was a very expensive silk, and I have n't worn it more than three or four times, and it really looks quite dowdy; and I can't get Patterson to do it over for me for this party. Well, really, I shall have to give up company because I have nothing to wear."

"Who *does* set the fashions, I wonder," said Humming-Bird; "they seem nowadays to whirl faster and faster, till really they don't leave one time for any-thing."

" Yes," said Dove, " I have n't a moment for reading, or drawing, or keeping up my music. The fact is, nowadays, to keep one's self properly dressed is all one can do. If I were *grande dame* now, and had only to send an order to my milliner and dressmaker, I might be beautifully dressed all the time without giving much thought to it myself; and that is what I should like. But this constant planning about one's toilet, changing your buttons and your fringes and your bonnet-trimmings and your hats every other day, and then being behindhand! It is really too fatiguing."

" Well," said Jennie, " I never pretend to keep up. I never expect to be in the front rank of fashion, but no girl wants to be behind every one ; nobody wants to have people say, ' Do see what an old-times, rubbishy looking creature *that* is.' And now, with my small means and my conscience, (for I have a conscience in this matter, and don't wish to spend any more time and money than is needed to keep one's self fresh and tasteful,) I find my dress quite a fatiguing care."

" Well, now, girls," said Humming-Bird, " do you really know, I have sometimes thought I should like to be a nun, just to get rid of all this labor. If I once gave up dress altogether, and knew I was to have nothing but one plain robe tied round my waist with a cord, it does seem to me as if it would be a perfect repose, — only one is a Protestant, you know."

Now, as Humming-Bird was the most notoriously dressy individual in the little circle, this suggestion was received with quite a laugh. But Dove took it up.

"Well, really," she said, "when dear Mr. S——— preaches those saintly sermons to us about our baptismal vows, and the nobleness of an unworldly life, and calls on us to live for something purer and higher than we are living for, I confess that sometimes all my life seems to me a mere sham, — that I am going to church, and saying solemn words, and being wrought up by solemn music, and uttering most solemn vows and prayers, all to no purpose ; and then I come away and look at my life, all resolving itself into a fritter about dress, and sewing-silk, cord, braid, and buttons, — the next fashion of bonnets, — how to make my old dresses answer instead of new, — how to keep the air of the world, while in my heart I am cherishing something higher and better. If there's anything I detest it is hypocrisy ; and sometimes the life I lead looks like it. But how to get out of it ? what to do ?"

"I'm sure," said Humming-Bird, "that taking care of my clothes and going into company is, frankly, *all* I do. If I go to parties, as other girls do, and make calls, and keep dressed, — you know papa is not rich,

N

and one must do these things economically, — it really does take all the time I have. When I was confirmed the Bishop talked to us so sweetly, and I really meant sincerely to be a good girl, — to be as good as I knew how ; but now, when they talk about fighting the good fight and running the Christian race, I feel very mean and little, for I am quite sure this is n't doing it. But what is, — and who is ? "

" Aunt Betsey Titcomb is doing it, I suppose," said Pheasant.

" Aunt Betsey ! " said Humming-Bird, " well, she is. She spends *all* her money in doing good. She goes round visiting the poor all the time. She is a perfect saint ; — but O girls, how she looks ! Well, now, I confess, when I think I must look like Aunt Betsey, my courage gives out. *Is* it necessary to go without hoops, and look like a dipped candle, in order to be unworldly ? Must one wear such a fright of a bonnet ? "

" No," said Jennie, " I think not. I think Miss Betsey Titcomb, good as she is, injures the cause of goodness by making it outwardly repulsive. I really think, if she would take some pains with her dress, and spend upon her own wardrobe a little of the money she gives away, that she might have influence in leading others to higher aims ; now all her influ-ence is against it. Her *outré* and repulsive exterior

arrays our natural and innocent feelings against goodness; for surely it is natural and innocent to wish to
look well, and I am really afraid a great many of us
are more afraid of being thought ridiculous than of
being wicked."

"And after all," said Pheasant, "you know Mr. St.
Clair says, 'Dress is one of the fine arts,' and if it
is, why of course we ought to cultivate it. Certainly,
well-dressed men and women are more agreeable objects than rude and unkempt ones. There must be
somebody whose mission it is to preside over the
agreeable arts of life; and I suppose it falls to 'us
girls.' That's the way I comfort myself, at all events.
Then I must confess that I do like dress; I'm not
cultivated enough to be a painter or a poet, and I have
all my artistic nature, such as it is, in dress. I love
harmonies of color, exact shades and matches; I love
to see a uniform idea carried all through a woman's
toilet, — her dress, her bonnet, her gloves, her shoes,
her pocket-handkerchief and cuffs, her very parasol,
all in correspondence."

"But my dear," said Jennie, "anything of this kind
must take a fortune!"

"And if I had a fortune, I'm pretty sure I should
spend a good deal of it in this way," said Pheasant.
"I can imagine such completeness of toilet as I have
never seen. How I would like the means to show

what I could do! My life, now, is perpetual disquiet. I always feel shabby. My things must all be bought at hap-hazard, as they can be got out of my poor little allowance, — and things are getting so horridly dear ! Only think of it, girls ! gloves at two and a quarter ! and boots at seven, eight, and ten dollars ! and then, as you say, the fashions changing so ! Why, I bought a sack last fall and gave forty dollars for it, and this winter I'm wearing it, to be sure, but it has no style at all, — looks quite antiquated ! "

"Now I say," said Jennie, " that you are really morbid on the subject of dress ; you are fastidious and particular and exacting in your ideas in a way that really ought to be put down. There is not a girl of our set that dresses as nicely as you do, except Emma Seyton, and her father, you know, has no end of income.'

" Nonsense, Jennie," said Pheasant. " I think I really look like a beggar ; but then, I bear it as well as I can, because, you see, I know papa does all for us he can, and I won't be extravagant. But I do think, as Humming-Bird says, that it would be a great relief to give it up altogether and retire from the world ; or, as Cousin John says, climb a tree and pull it up after you, and so be in peace."

"Well," said Jennie, " all this seems to have come on since the war. It seems to me that not only has everything doubled in price, but all the habits of the would seem to require that you shall have double the quantity of everything. Two or three years ago a good balmoral skirt was a fixed fact ; it was a convenient thing for sloppy, unpleasant weather. But now, dear me ! there is no end to them. They cost fifteen and twenty dollars ; and girls that I know have one or two every season, besides all sorts of quilled and embroidered and ruffled and tucked and flounced ones. Then, in dressing one's hair, what a perfect overflow there is of all manner of waterfalls, and braids, and rats and mice, and curls, and combs ; when three or four years ago we combed our own hair innocently behind our ears, and put flowers in it, and thought we looked nicely at our evening parties ! I don't believe we look any better now, when we are dressed, than we did then, — so what 's the use ? "

" Well, did you ever see such a tyranny as this of fashion ? " said Humming-Bird. " We know it 's silly, but we all bow down before it ; we are afraid of our lives before it ; and who makes all this and sets it going? The Paris milliners, the Empress, or who ? "

" The question where fashions come from is like the question where pins go to," said Pheasant. " Think of the thousands and millions of pins that are being used every year, and not one of them worn out. Where do they all go to ? One would expect to find a pin mine somewhere."

"Victor Hugo says they go into the sewers in Paris," said Jennie.

"And the fashions come from a source about as pure," said I, from the next room.

"Bless me, Jennie, do tell us if your father has been listening to us all this time!" was the next exclamation ; and forthwith there was a whir and rustle of the silken wings, as the whole troop fluttered into my study.

"Now, Mr. Crowfield, you are too bad!" said Humming-Bird, as she perched upon a corner of my study-table, and put her little feet upon an old "Frois sart" which filled the arm-chair.

"To be listening to our nonsense!" said Pheasant.

"Lying in wait for us!" said Dove.

"Well, now, you have brought us all down on you," said Humming-Bird, "and you won't find it so easy to be rid of us.   You will have to answer all our questions."

"My dears, I am at your service, as far as mortal man may be," said I.

"Well, then," said Humming-Bird, "tell us all about everything, — how things come to be as they are.   Who makes the fashions?"

"I believe it is universally admitted that, in the matter of feminine toilet, France rules the world, said I.

"But who rules France?" said Pheasant. "Who decides what the fashions shall be there?"

"It is the great misfortune of the civilized world, at the present hour," said I, " that the state of morals in France is apparently at the very lowest ebb, and consequently the leadership of fashion is entirely in the hands of a class of women who could not be admitted into good society, in any country. Women who can never have the name of wife, — who know none of the ties of family, — these are the dictators whose dress and equipage and appointments give the law, first to France, and through France to the civilized world. Such was the confession of Monsieur Dupin, made in a late speech before the French Senate, and acknowledged, with murmurs of assent on all sides, to be the truth. This is the reason why the fashions have such an utter disregard of all those laws of prudence and economy which regulate the expenditures of families. They are made by women whose sole and only hold on life is personal attractiveness, and with whom to keep this up, at any cost, is a desperate necessity. No moral quality, no association of purity, truth, modesty, self-denial, or family love, comes in to hallow the atmosphere about them, and create a sphere of loveliness which brightens as mere physical beauty fades. The ravages of time and dissipation must be made up by an unceasing study of the arts of the toilet. Artists of all sorts, moving in their train, rack all the stores of ancient and modern art for the picturesque, the dazzling, the grotesque ; and so, lest these Circes of society should carry all before them, and enchant every husband, brother, and lover, the staid and lawful Penelopes leave the hearth and home to follow in their triumphal march and imitate their arts. Thus it goes in France ; and in England, virtuous and domestic princesses and peeresses must take obediently what has been decreed by their rulers in the *demi-monde* of France ; and we in America have leaders of fashion, who make it their pride and glory to turn New York into Paris, and to keep even step with everything that is going on there. So the whole world of woman-kind is marching under the command of these leaders. The love of dress and glitter and fashion is getting to be a morbid, unhealthy epidemic, which really eats away the nobleness and purity of women.

"In France, as Monsieur Dupin, Edmond About, and Michelet tell us, the extravagant demands of love for dress lead women to contract debts unknown to their husbands, and sign obligations which are paid by the sacrifice of honor, and thus the purity of the family is continually undermined. In England there is a voice of complaint, sounding from the leading periodicals, that the extravagant demands of female fashion are bringing distress into families, and making marriages impossible ; and something of the same sort seems to have begun here. We are across the Atlantic, to be sure ; but we feel the swirl and drift of the great whirlpool ; only, fortunately, we are far enough off to be able to see whither things are tending, and to stop ourselves if we will.

" We have just come through a great struggle, in which our women have borne an heroic part, — have shown themselves capable of any kind of endurance and self-sacrifice ; and now we are in that reconstructive state which makes it of the greatest consequence to ourselves and the world that we understand our own institutions and position, and learn that, instead of following the corrupt and worn-out ways of the Old World, we are called on to set the example of a new state of society, — noble, simple, pure, and religious ; and women can do more towards this even than men, for women are the real architects of society.

" Viewed in this light, even the small, frittering cares of woman's life — the attention to buttons, trimmings, thread, and sewing-silk — may be an expression of their patriotism and their religion. A noble-hearted woman puts a noble meaning into even the commonplace details of life. The women of America can, if they choose, hold back their country from following in the wake of old, corrupt, worn-out, effeminate

10

European society, and make America the leader of the world in all that is good."

"I'm sure," said Humming-Bird, "we all would like to be noble and heroic. During the war, I did so long to be a man! I felt so poor and insignificant because I was nothing but a girl!"

"Ah, well," said Pheasant, "but then one wants to do something worth doing, if one is going to do anything. One would like to be grand and heroic, if one could; but if not, why try at all? One wants to be *very* something, *very* great, *very* heroic; or if not that, then at least very stylish and very fashionable. It is this everlasting mediocrity that bores me."

"Then, I suppose, you agree with the man we read of, who buried his one talent in the earth, as hardly worth caring for."

"To say the truth, I always had something of a sympathy for that man," said Pheasant. "I can't enjoy goodness and heroism in homœopathic doses. I want something appreciable. What I can do, being a woman, is a very different thing from what I should try to do if I were a man, and had a man's chances: it is so much less — so poor — that it is scarcely worth trying for."

"You remember," said I, "the apothegm of one of the old divines, that if two angels were sent down from heaven, the one to govern a kingdom, and the other to sweep a street, they would not feel any disposition to change works."

"Well, that just shows that they are angels, and not mortals," said Pheasant; "but we poor human beings see things differently."

"Yet, my child, what could Grant or Sherman have done, if it had not been for the thousands of brave privates who were content to do each their imperceptible little, — if it had not been for the poor, unnoticed, faithful, never-failing common soldiers, who did the work and bore the suffering? No *one* man saved our country, or could save it; nor could the men have saved it without the women. Every mother that said to her son, Go ; every wife that strengthened the hands of her husband ; every girl who sent courageous letters to her betrothed ; every woman who worked for a fair ; every grandam whose trembling hands knit stockings and scraped lint; every little maiden who hemmed shirts and made comfort-bags for soldiers, — each and all have been the joint doers of a great heroic work, the doing of which has been the regeneration of our era. A whole generation has learned the luxury of thinking heroic thoughts and being conversant with heroic deeds, and I have faith to believe that all this is not to go out in a mere crush of fashionable luxury and folly and frivolous emptiness, — but that our girls are going to merit the high praise given us by De Tocqueville, when he placed first among the causes of our prosperity the *noble character of American women.* Because foolish female persons in New York are striving to outdo the *demi-monde* of Paris in extravagance, it must not follow that every sensible and patriotic matron, and every nice, modest young girl, must forthwith, and without inquiry, rush as far after them as they possibly can. Because Mrs. Shoddy opens a ball in a two-thousand-dollar lace dress, every girl in the land need not look with shame on her modest white muslin. Somewhere between the fast women of Paris and the daughters of Christian American families there should be established a *cordon sanitaire,* to keep out the contagion of manners, customs, and habits with which a noble-minded, religious democratic people ought to have nothing to lo."

"Well now, Mr. Crowfield," said the Dove, "since you speak us so fair, and expect so much of us, we must of course try not to fall below your compliments; but, after all, tell us what is the right standard about dress. Now we have daily lectures about this at home. Aunt Maria says that she never saw such times as these, when mothers and daughters, church-members and worldly people, all seem to be going one way, and sit down together and talk, as they will, on dress and fashion, — how to have this made and that altered. We used to be taught, she said, that church-members had higher things to think of, — that their thoughts ought to be fixed on something better, and that they ought to restrain the vanity and worldliness of children and young people ; but now, she says, even before a girl is born, dress is the one thing needful, — the great thing to be thought of ; and so, in every step of the way upward, her little shoes, and her little bonnets, and her little dresses, and her corals and her ribbons, are constantly being discussed in her presence, as the one all-important object of life. Aunt Maria thinks mamma is dreadful, because she has maternal yearnings over our toilet successes and fortunes ; and we secretly think Aunt Maria is rather soured by old age, and has forgotten how a girl feels."

" The fact is," said I, " that the love of dress and outside show has been always such an exacting and absorbing tendency, that it seems to have furnished work for religionists and economists, in all ages, to keep it within bounds. Various religious bodies, at the outset, adopted severe rules in protest against it. The Quakers and the Methodists prescribed certain fixed modes of costume as a barrier against its frivolities and follies. In the Romish Church an entrance on any religious order prescribed entire and total renunciation of all thought and care for the beautiful

in person or apparel, as the first step towards saint
ship. The costume of the *religieuse* seemed to be
purposely intended to imitate the shroudings and
swathings of a corpse and the lugubrious color of a
pall, so as forever to remind the wearer that she was
dead to the world of ornament and physical beauty.
All great Christian preachers and reformers have
levelled their artillery against the toilet, from the time
of St. Jerome downward ; and Tom Moore has put
into beautiful and graceful verse St. Jerome's admoni-
tions to the fair church-goers of his time.

'WHO IS THE MAID?

'ST. JEROME'S LOVE.

' Who is the maid my spirit seeks,
 Through cold reproof and slander's **blight ?**
Has *she* Love's roses on her cheeks ?
 Is *hers* an eye of this world's light ?
No : wan and sunk with midnight **prayer**
 Are the pale looks of her I love ;
Or if, at times, a light be there,
 Its beam is kindled from above.

'I chose not her, my heart's elect,
 From those who seek their Maker's **shrine**
In gems and garlands proudly decked,
 As if themselves were things divine.
No : Heaven but faintly warms the **breast**
 That beats beneath a broidered veil ;

And she who comes in glittering vest
    To mourn her frailty still is frail.

'Not so the faded form I prize
    And love, because its bloom is **gone ;**
The glory in those sainted eyes
    Is all the grace *her* brow puts on.
And ne'er was Beauty's dawn so bright,
    So touching, as that form's decay,
Which, like the altar's trembling light,
    In holy lustre wastes away.'

"But the defect of all these modes of warfare on the elegances and refinements of the toilet was that they were too indiscriminate. They were in reality founded on a false principle. They took for granted that there was something radically corrupt and wicked in the body and in the physical system. According to this mode of viewing things, the body was a loath-some and pestilent prison, in which the soul was locked up and enslaved, and the eyes, the ears, the taste, the smell, were all so many corrupt traitors in conspiracy to poison her. Physical beauty of every sort was a snare, a Circean enchantment, to be valiantly contended with and straitly eschewed. Hence they preached, not moderation, but total abstinence from all pursuit of physical grace and beauty.

"Now, a resistance founded on an over-statement

is constantly tending to reaction.   People always have a tendency to begin thinking for themselves ; and when they so think, they perceive that a good and wise God would not have framed our bodies with such exquisite care only to corrupt our souls, — that physical beauty, being created in such profuse abundance around us, and we being possessed with such a longing for it, must have its uses, its legitimate sphere of exercise.   Even the poor, shrouded nun, as she walks the convent garden, cannot help asking herself why, if the crimson velvet of the rose was made by God, all colors except black and white are sinful for her ; and the modest Quaker, after hanging all her house and dressing all her children in drab, cannot but marvel at the sudden outstreaking of blue and yellow and crimson in the tulip-beds under her window, and reflect how very differently the great All-Father arrays the world's housekeeping.   The consequence of all this has been, that the reforms based upon these severe and exclusive views have gradually gone backward.   The Quaker dress is imperceptibly and gracefully melting away into a refined simplicity of modern costume, which in many cases seems to be the perfection of taste.   The obvious reflection, that one color of the rainbow is quite as much of God as another, has led the children of gentle dove-colored mothers to appear in shades of rose-color, blue, and lilac; and wise elders have said, it is not so much the color or the shape that we object to, as giving too much time and too much money, — if the heart be right with God and man, the bonnet ribbon may be of any shade you please."

"But don't you think," said Pheasant, "that a certain fixed dress, marking the unworldly character of a religious order, is desirable? Now, I have said before that I am very fond of dress. I have a passion for beauty and completeness in it; and as long as I am in the world and obliged to dress as the world does, it constantly haunts me, and tempts me to give more time, more thought, more money, to these things than I really think they are worth. But I can conceive of giving up this thing altogether as being much easier than regulating it to the precise point. I never read of a nun's taking the veil, without a certain thrill of sympathy. To cut off one's hair, to take off and cast from her, one by one, all one's trinkets and jewels, to lie down and have the pall thrown over one, and feel one's self, once for all, dead to the world, — I cannot help feeling as if this were real, thorough, noble renunciation, and as if one might rise up from it with a grand, calm consciousness of having risen to a higher and purer atmosphere, and got above all the littlenesses and distractions that beset us here. So I have heard charming young

10*   o

Quaker girls, who, in more thoughtless days, indulged in what for them was a slight shading of worldly conformity, say that it was to them a blessed rest when they put on the strict, plain dress, and felt that they really had taken up the cross and turned their backs on the world. I can conceive of doing this, much more easily than I can of striking the exact line between worldly conformity and noble aspiration, in the life I live now."

"My dear child," said I, "we all overlook one great leading principle of our nature, and that is, that we are made to find a higher pleasure in self-sacrifice than in any form of self-indulgence. There is something grand and pathetic in the idea of an entire self-surrender, to which every human soul leaps up, as we do to the sound of martial music.

"How many boys of Boston and New York, who had lived effeminate and idle lives, felt this new power uprising in them in our war! How they embraced the dirt and discomfort and fatigue and watchings and toils of camp-life with an eagerness of zest which they had never felt in the pursuit of mere pleasure, and wrote home burning letters that they never were so happy in their lives! It was not that dirt and fatigue and discomfort and watchings and weariness were in themselves agreeable, but it was a joy to feel themselves able to bear all and surrender all for something higher than self. Many a poor Battery bully of New York, many a street rowdy, felt uplifted by the discovery that he too had hid away under the dirt and dust of his former life this divine and precious jewel. He leaped for joy to find that he too could be a hero. Think of the hundreds of thousands of plain, ordinary workingmen, and of seemingly ordinary boys, who, but for such a crisis, might have passed through life never knowing this to be in them, and who courageously endured hunger and thirst and cold, and separation from dearest friends, for days and weeks and months, when they might, at any day, have bought a respite by deserting their country's flag! Starving boys, sick at heart, dizzy in head, pining for home and mother, still found warmth and comfort in the one thought that they could suffer, die, for their country; and the graves at Salisbury and Andersonville show in how many souls this noble power of self-sacrifice to the higher good was lodged, — how many there were, even in the humblest walks of life, who preferred death by torture to life in dishonor.

" It is this heroic element in man and woman that makes self-sacrifice an ennobling and purifying ordeal in any religious profession. The man really is taken into a higher region of his own nature, and finds a pleasure in the exercise of higher faculties which he did not suppose himself to possess. Whatever sacrifice is supposed to be duty, whether the supposition be really correct or not, has in it an ennobling and purifying power; and thus the eras of conversion from one form of the Christian religion to another are often marked with a real and permanent exaltation of the whole character. But it does not follow that certain religious beliefs and ordinances are in themselves just, because they thus touch the great heroic master-chord of the human soul. To wear sackcloth and sleep on a plank may have been of use to many souls, as symbolizing the awakening of this higher nature; but, still, the religion of the New Testament is plainly one which calls to no such outward and evident sacrifices.

"It was John the Baptist, and not the Messiah, who dwelt in the wilderness and wore garments of camel's hair; and Jesus was commented on, not for his asceticism, but for his cheerful, social acceptance of the average innocent wants and enjoyments of humanity. 'The Son of man came eating and drinking.' The great, and never-ceasing, and utter self-sacrifice of his life was not signified by any peculiarity of costume, or language, or manner; it showed itself only as it unconsciously welled up in all his words and actions, in his estimates of life, in all that marked him out as a being of a higher and holier sphere."

"Then you do not believe in influencing this sub

ject of dress by religious persons' adopting any particular laws of costume?" said Pheasant.

"I do not see it to be possible," said I, "considering how society is made up. There are such differences of taste and character, — people move in such different spheres, are influenced by such different circumstances, — that all we can do is to lay down certain great principles, and leave it to every one to apply them according to individual needs."

"But what are these principles? There is the grand inquiry."

"Well," said I, "let us feel our way. In the first place, then, we are all agreed in one starting-point, — that beauty is not to be considered as a bad thing, — that the love of ornament in our outward and physical life is not a sinful or a dangerous feeling, and only leads to evil, as all other innocent things do, by being used in wrong ways. So far we are all agreed, are we not?"

"Certainly," said all the voices.

"It is, therefore, neither wicked nor silly nor weak-minded to like beautiful dress, and all that goes to make it up. Jewelry, diamonds, pearls, emeralds, rubies, and all sorts of pretty things that are made of them, are as lawful and innocent objects of admiration and desire, as flowers or birds or butterflies, or the tints of evening skies. Gems, in fact, are a species of mineral flower; they are the blossoms of the dark, hard mine; and what they want in perfume they make up in durability. The best Christian in the world may, without the least inconsistency, admire them, and say, as a charming, benevolent old Quaker lady once said to me, 'I do so love to look at beautiful jewelry!' The love of beautiful dress, in itself, therefore, so far from being in a bad sense worldly, may be the same indication of a refined and poetical nature that is given by the love of flowers and of natural objects.

"In the third place, there is nothing in itself wrong, or unworthy a rational being, in a certain degree of attention to the fashion of society in our costume. It is not wrong to be annoyed at unnecessary departures from the commonly received practices of good society in the matter of the arrangement of our toilet; and it would indicate rather an unamiable want of sympathy with our fellow-beings, if we were not willing, for the most part, to follow what they indicate to be agreeable in the disposition of our outward affairs."

"Well, I must say, Mr. Crowfield, you are allowing us all a very generous margin," said Humming-Bird.

"But, now," said I, "I am coming to the restrictions. When is love of dress excessive and wrong? To this I answer by stating my faith in one of old Plato's ideas, in which he speaks of beauty and its uses. He says there were two impersonations of

beauty worshipped under the name of Venus in the
ancient times, — the one celestial, born of the highest
gods, the other earthly. To the earthly Venus the
sacrifices were such as were more trivial; to the celestial, such as were more holy. 'The worship of the
earthly Venus,' he says, 'sends us oftentimes on unworthy and trivial errands, but the worship of the
celestial to high and honorable friendships, to noble
aspirations and heroic actions.'

"Now it seems to me that, if we bear in mind this
truth in regard to beauty, we shall have a test with
which to try ourselves in the matter of physical adornment. We are always excessive when we sacrifice the
higher beauty to attain the lower one. A woman who
will sacrifice domestic affection, conscience, self-respect, honor, to love of dress, we all agree, loves dress
too much. She loses the true and higher beauty of
womanhood for the lower beauty of gems and flowers
and colors. A girl who sacrifices to dress all her time,
all her strength, all her money, to the neglect of the
cultivation of her mind and heart, and to the neglect
of the claims of others on her helpfulness, is sacrific-
ing the higher to the lower beauty. Her fault is not
the love of beauty, but loving the wrong and inferior
kind.

"It is remarkable that the directions of Holy Writ,
in regard to the female dress, should distinctly **take**

note of this difference between the higher and the lower beauty which we find in the works of Plato. The Apostle gives no rule, no specific costume, which should mark the Christian woman from the Pagan; but says, 'whose adorning, let it not be that outward adorning of plaiting the hair, and of wearing of gold, or of putting on of apparel; but let it be the hidden man of the heart, in that which is not corruptible, even the ornament of a meek and quiet spirit, which is in the sight of God of great price.' The gold and gems and apparel are not forbidden; but we are told not to depend on them for beauty, to the neglect of those imperishable, immortal graces that belong to the soul. The makers of fashion among whom Christian women lived when the Apostle wrote were the same class of brilliant and worthless Aspasias who make the fashions of modern Paris; and all womankind was sunk into slavish adoration of mere physical adornment when the Gospel sent forth among them this call to the culture of a higher and immortal beauty.

"In fine, girls," said I, "you may try yourselves by this standard. You love dress too much when you care more for your outward adornings than for your inward dispositions, — when it afflicts you more to have torn your dress than to have lost your temper, — when you are more troubled by an ill-fitting gown

than by a neglected duty, — when you are less con-
cerned at having made an unjust comment, or spread
a scandalous report, than at having worn a *passée* bonnet, — when you are less troubled at the thought of
being found at the last great feast without the wedding
garment, than at being found at the party to-night in
the fashion of last year. No Christian woman, as I
view it, ought to give such attention to her dress as to
allow it to take up *all* of three very important things,
viz. : —

All her time.

All her strength.

All her money.

Whoever does this lives not the Christian, but the
Pagan life, — worships not at the Christian's altar of
our Lord Jesus, but at the shrine of the lower Venus
of Corinth and Rome."

"O now, Mr. Crowfield, you frighten me," said
Humming-Bird. "I'm so afraid, do you know, that
I am doing exactly that."

"And so am I," said Pheasant; "and yet, certainly,
it is not what I mean or intend to do."

"But how to help it," said Dove.

"My dears," said I, "where there is a will there is
a way. Only resolve that you will put the true beauty
first, — that, even if you do have to seem unfashion-
able, you will follow the highest beauty of woman-

hood, — and the battle is half gained. Only resolve that your time, your strength, your money, such as you have, shall not all — nor more than half — be given to mere outward adornment, and you will go right. It requires only an army of girls animated with this noble purpose to declare independence in America, and emancipate us from the decrees and tyrannies of French actresses and ballet-dancers. *En avant*, girls! You yet can, if you will, save the republic."

X.

WHAT ARE THE SOURCES OF BEAUTY IN DRESS.

THE conversation on dress which I had held with Jennie and her little covey of Birds of Paradise appeared to have worked in the minds of the fair council, for it was not long before they invaded my study again in a body. They were going out to a party, but called for Jennie, and of course gave me and Mrs. Crowfield the privilege of seeing them equipped for conquest.

Latterly, I must confess, the mysteries of the toilet rites have impressed me with a kind of superstitious awe. Only a year ago my daughter Jennie had smooth dark hair, which she wreathed in various soft, flowing lines about her face, and confined in a classical knot on the back of her head. Jennie had rather a talent for *coiffure*, and the arrangement of her hair was one of my little artistic delights. She always had something there, — a leaf, a spray, a bud or blossom, that looked fresh, and had a sort of poetical grace of its own.

But in a gradual way all this has been changing. Jennie's him first became slightly wavy, then curly, finally frizzly, presenting a tumbled and twisted appearance, which gave me great inward concern; but when I spoke upon the subject I was always laughingly silenced with the definitive settling remark: "O, it's the fashion, papa! Everybody wears it so."

I particularly objected to the change on my own small account, because the smooth, breakfast-table *coiffure*, which I had always so much enjoyed, was now often exchanged for a peculiarly bristling appearance; the hair being variously twisted, tortured, woven, and wound, without the least view to immediate beauty or grace. But all this, I was informed, was the necessary means towards crimping for some evening display of a more elaborate nature than usual.

Mrs. Crowfield and myself are not party-goers by profession, but Jennie insists on our going out at least once or twice in a season, just, as she says, to keep up with the progress of society; and at these times I have been struck with frequent surprise by the general untidiness which appeared to have come over the heads of all my female friends. I know, of course, that I am only a poor, ignorant, bewildered man-creature; but to my uninitiated eyes they looked as if they had all, after a very restless and perturbed

sleep, come out of bed without smoothing their tumbled and disordered locks. Then, every young lady,
without exception, seemed to have one kind of hair,
and that the kind which was rather suggestive of the
term *woolly*. Every sort of wild *abandon* of frowzy
locks seemed to be in vogue; in some cases the hair
appearing to my vision nothing but a confused snarl,
in which glittered tinklers, spangles, and bits of tinsel, and from which waved long pennants and streamers of different-colored ribbons.

I was in fact very greatly embarrassed by my first
meeting with some very charming girls, whom I
thought I knew as familiarly as my own daughter
Jennie, and whose soft, pretty hair had often formed
the object of my admiration. Now, however, they
revealed themselves to me in *coiffures* which forcibly
reminded me of the electrical experiments which used
to entertain us in college, when the subject stood on
the insulated stool, and each particular hair of his
head bristled and rose, and set up, as it were, on its
own account. This high-flying condition of the tress-
es, and the singularity of the ornaments which appeared to be thrown at hap-hazard into them, suggested so oddly the idea of a bewitched person, that I
could scarcely converse with any presence of mind,
or realize that these really were the nice, well-in-
formed, sensible little girls of my own neighborhood,

— the good daughters, good sisters, Sunday-school teachers, and other familiar members of our best educated circles ; and I came away from the party in a sort of blue maze, and hardly in a state to conduct myself with credit in the examination through which I knew Jennie would put me as to the appearance of her different friends.

I know not how it is, but the glamour of fashion in the eyes of girlhood is so complete, that the oddest, wildest, most uncouth devices find grace and favor in the eyes of even well-bred girls, when once that invisible, ineffable *aura* has breathed over them which declares them to be fashionable. They may defy them for a time, — they may pronounce them horrid ; but it is with a secretly melting heart, and with a mental reservation to look as nearly like the abhorred spectacle as they possibly can on the first favorable opportunity.

On the occasion of the visit referred to, Jennie ushered her three friends in triumph into my study ; and, in truth, the little room seemed to be perfectly transformed by their brightness. My honest, nice, lovable little Yankee-fireside girls were, to be sure, got up in a style that would have done credit to Madame Pompadour, or any of the most questionable characters of the time of Louis XIV. or XV. They were frizzled and powdered, and built up in elaborate

devices; they wore on their hair flowers, gems,
streamers, tinklers, humming-birds, butterflies, South
American beetles, beads, bugles, and all imaginable
rattle-traps, which jingled and clinked with every
motion; and yet, as they were three or four fresh,
handsome, intelligent, bright-eyed girls, there was no
denying the fact that they *did look extremely pretty;*
and as they sailed hither and thither before me, and
gazed down upon me in the saucy might of their rosy
girlhood, there was a gay defiance in Jennie's demand,
" Now, papa, how do you like us ? "

" Very charming," answered I, surrendering at discretion.

" I told you, girls, that you could convert him to
the fashions, if he should once see you in party trim."

" I beg pardon, my dear; I am not converted to
the fashion, but to you, and that is a point on which
I did n't need conversion ; but the present fashions,
even so fairly represented as I see them, I humbly
confess I dislike."

" O Mr. Crowfield ! "

" Yes, my dears, I do. But then, I protest, I 'm
not fairly treated. I think, for a young American
girl, who looks as most of my fair friends do look, to
come down with her bright eyes and all her little pan-
oply of graces upon an old fellow like me, and expect
him to like a fashion merely because *she* looks well

in it, is all sheer nonsense. Why, girls, if you wore rings in your noses, and bangles on your arms up to your elbows, if you tied your hair in a war-knot on the top of your heads like the Sioux Indians, you would look pretty still. The question is n't, as I view it, whether you look pretty, — for that you do, and that you will, do what you please and dress how you will. The question is whether you might not look prettier, whether another style of dress, and another mode of getting up, would not be far more becoming. I am one who thinks that it would."

"Now, Mr. Crowfield, you positively are too bad," said Humming-Bird, whose delicate head was encircled by a sort of crapy cloud of bright hair, sparkling with gold-dust and spangles, in the midst of which, just over her forehead, a gorgeous blue butterfly was perched, while a confused mixture of hairs, gold-powder, spangles, stars, and tinkling ornaments fell in a sort of cataract down her pretty neck. "You see, we girls think everything of you; and now we don't like it that you don't like our fashions."

"Why, my little princess, so long as I like *you* better than your fashions, and merely think they are not worthy of you, what's the harm?"

"O yes, to be sure. You sweeten the dose to us babies with that sugar-plum. But really, Mr. Crowfield, why don't you like the fashions?"

"Because, to my view, they are in great part in false taste, and injure the beauty of the girls," said I. "They are inappropriate to their characters, and make them look like a kind and class of women whom they do not, and I trust never will, resemble internally, and whose mark therefore they ought not to bear externally. But there you are, beguiling me into a sermon which you will only hate me in your hearts for preaching. Go along, children! You certainly look as well as anybody can in that style of getting up; so go to your party, and to-morrow night, when you are tired and sleepy, if you'll come with your crochet, and sit in my study, I will read you Christopher Crowfield's dissertation on dress."

"That will be amusing, to say the least," said Humming-Bird; "and, be sure, we will all be here. And mind, you have to show good reasons for disliking the present fashion."

So the next evening there was a worsted party in my study, sitting in the midst of which I read as follows :

"WHAT ARE THE SOURCES OF BEAUTY IN DRESS.

"The first one is *appropriateness*. Colors and forms and modes, in themselves graceful or beautiful, can become ungraceful and ridiculous simply through inappropriateness. The most lovely bonnet that the most approved *modiste* can invent, if worn on the head of a coarse-faced Irishwoman bearing a market-basket on her arm, excites no emotion but that of the ludicrous. The most elegant and brilliant evening dress, if worn in the daytime in a railroad car, strikes every one with a sense of absurdity; whereas both these objects in appropriate associations would excite only the idea of beauty. So, a mode of dress obviously intended for driving strikes us as *outré* in a parlor; and a parlor dress would no less shock our eyes on horseback. In short, the course of this principle through all varieties of form can easily be perceived. Besides appropriateness to time, place, and circumstances, there is appropriateness to age, position, and character. This is the foundation of all our ideas of professional propriety in costume. One would not like to see a clergyman in his external air and appointments resembling a gentleman of the turf; one would not wish a refined and modest scholar to wear the outward air of a fast fellow, or an aged and venerable statesman to appear with all the peculiarities of a young dandy. The flowers, feathers, and furbelows which a light-hearted young girl of seventeen embellishes by the airy grace with which she wears them, are simply ridiculous when transferred to the toilet of her serious, well-meaning mamma, who bears them about with an anxious face, merely because a loqua-

cious milliner· has assured her, with many protesta-
tions, that it is the fashion, and the only thing remain-
ing for her to do.

"There are, again, modes of dress in themselves
very beautiful and very striking, which are peculiarly
adapted to theatrical representation and to pictures,
but the adoption of which as a part of unprofessional
toilet produces a sense of incongruity. A mode of
dress may be in perfect taste on the stage, that would
be absurd in an evening party, absurd in the street,
absurd, in short, everywhere else.

"Now you come to my first objection to our present American toilet, — its being to a very great extent
inappropriate to our climate, to our habits of life and
thought, and to the whole structure of ideas on which
our life is built. What we want, apparently, is some
court of inquiry and adaptation that shall pass judgment on the fashions of other countries, and modify
them to make them a graceful expression of our own
national character, and modes of thinking and living.
A certain class of women in Paris at this present hour
makes the fashions that rule the feminine world.
They are women who live only for the senses, with as
utter and obvious disregard of any moral or intellectual purpose to be answered in living as a paroquet or
a macaw. They have no family ties; love, in its pure
domestic sense, is an impossibility in their lot; re-

ligion in any sense is another impossibility; and their
whole intensity of existence, therefore, is concentrated
on the question of sensuous enjoyment, and that
personal adornment which is necessary to secure it.
When the great, ruling country in the world of taste
and fashion has fallen into such a state that the vir-
tual leaders of fashion are women of this character, it
is not to be supposed that the fashions emanating from
them will be of a kind well adapted to express the
ideas, the thoughts, the state of society, of a great
Christian democracy such as ours ought to be.

"What is called, for example, the Pompadour style
of dress, so much in vogue of late, we can see to be
perfectly adapted to the kind of existence led by dissipated women, whose life is one revel of excitement;
and who, never proposing to themselves any intellectual employment or any domestic duty, can afford to
spend three or four hours every day under the hands
of a waiting-maid, in alternately tangling and untang-
ling their hair.   Powder, paint, gold-dust and silver-
dust, pomatums, cosmetics, are all perfectly appropriate where the ideal of life is to keep up a false
show of beauty after the true bloom is wasted by
dissipation.   The woman who never goes to bed till
morning, who never even dresses herself, who never
takes a needle in her hand, who never goes to church,
and never entertains one serious idea of duty of any

kind, when got up in Pompadour style, has, to say the truth, the good taste and merit of appropriateness. Her dress expresses just what she is, — all false, all artificial, all meretricious and unnatural; no part or portion of her from which it might be inferred what her Creator originally designed her to be.

"But when a nice little American girl, who has been brought up to cultivate her mind, to refine her taste, to care for her health, to be a helpful daughter and a good sister, to visit the poor and teach in Sunday schools; when a good, sweet, modest little puss of this kind combs all her pretty hair backward till it is one mass of frowzy confusion; when she powders, and paints under her eyes; when she adopts, with eager enthusiasm, every *outré*, unnatural fashion that comes from the most dissipated foreign circles, — she is in bad taste, because she does not represent either her character, her education, or her good points. She looks like a second-rate actress, when she is, in fact, a most thoroughly respectable, estimable, lovable little girl, and on the way, as we poor fellows fondly hope, to bless some one of us with her tenderness and care in some nice home in the future.

"It is not the fashion in America for young girls to nave waiting-maids, — in foreign countries it is the fashion. All this meretricious toilet — so elaborate, so complicated, and so contrary to nature — must be accomplished, and is accomplished, by the busy little fingers of each girl for herself; and so it seems to be very evident that a style of hair-dressing which it will require hours to disentangle, which must injure and in time ruin the natural beauty of the hair, ought to be one thing which a well-regulated court of inquiry would reject in our American fashions.

"Again, the genius of American life is for simplicity and absence of ostentation. We have no parade of office ; our public men wear no robes, no stars, garters, collars, &c. ; and it would, therefore, be in good taste in our women to cultivate simple styles of dress. Now I object to the present fashions, as adopted from France, that they are flashy and theatrical. Having their origin with a community whose senses are blunted, drugged, and deadened with dissipation and ostentation, they reject the simpler forms of beauty, and seek for startling effects, for odd and unexpected results. The contemplation of one of our fashionable churches, at the hour when its fair occupants pour forth, gives one a great deal of surprise. The toilet there displayed might have been n good keeping among showy Parisian women in an opera-house ; but even their original inventors would have been shocked at the idea of carrying them into a church. The rawness of our American mind as to the subject of propriety in dress is nowhere more shown than in the fact that no apparent distinction is made between church and opera-house in the adaptation of attire. Very estimable, and, we trust, very religious young women sometimes enter the house of God in a costume which makes their utterance of the words of the litany and the acts of prostrate devotion in the service seem almost burlesque. When a brisk little creature comes into a pew with hair frizzed till it stands on end in a most startling manner, rattling strings of beads and bits of tinsel, mounting over all some pert little hat with a red or green feather standing saucily upright in front, she may look exceedingly pretty and *piquante;* and, if she came there for a game of croquet or a tableau-party, would be all in very good taste; but as she comes to confess that she is a miserable sinner, that she has done the things she ought not to have done and left undone the things she ought to have done, — as she takes upon her lips most solemn and tremendous words, whose meaning runs far beyond life into a sublime eternity, — there is a discrepancy which would be ludicrous if it were not melancholy.

"One is apt to think, at first view, that St. Jerome was right in saying,

'She who comes in glittering veil
To mourn her frailty, still is frail.'

But St. Jerome was in the wrong, after all; for a

flashy, unsuitable attire in church is not always a mark of an undevout or entirely worldly mind; it is simply a mark of a raw, uncultivated taste. In Italy, the ecclesiastical law prescribing a uniform black dress for the churches gives a sort of education to European ideas of propriety in toilet, which prevents churches from being made theatres for the same kind of display which is held to be in good taste at places of public amusement. It is but justice to the inventors of Parisian fashions to say, that, had they ever had the smallest idea of going to church and Sunday school, as our good girls do, they would immediately have devised toilets appropriate to such exigencies. If it were any part of their plan of life to appear statedly in public to confess themselves 'miserable sinners,' we should doubtless have sent over here the design of some graceful penitential habit, which would give our places of worship a much more appropriate air than they now have. As it is, it would form a subject for such a court of inquiry and adaptation as we have supposed, to draw a line between the costume of the theatre and the church.

"In the same manner, there is a want of appropriateness in the costume of our American women, who display in the street promenade a style of dress and adornment originally intended for showy carriage drives in such great exhibition grounds as the Bois de

Boulogne. The makers of Parisian fashions are not
generally walkers. They do not, with all their extravagance, have the bad taste to trail yards of silk
and velvet over the mud and dirt of a pavement,
or promenade the street in a costume so pronounced
and striking as to draw the involuntary glance of
every eye ; and the showy toilets displayed on the
pavé by American young women have more than once
exposed them to misconstruction in the eyes of foreign observers.

"Next to appropriateness, the second requisite to
beauty in dress I take to be unity of effect. In
speaking of the arrangement of rooms in the ' House
and Home Papers,' I criticised some apartments
wherein were many showy articles of furniture, and
much expense had been incurred, because, with all
this, there was no *unity of result.* The carpet was
costly, and in itself handsome ; the paper was also in
itself handsome and costly ; the tables and chairs
also in themselves very elegant ; and yet, owing to
a want of any unity of idea, any grand harmonizing
tint of color, or method of arrangement, the rooms
had a jumbled, confused air, and nothing about them
seemed particularly pretty or effective. I instanced
rooms where thousands of dollars had been spent,
which, because of this defect, never excited admiration ; and others in which the furniture was of the

11 *

cheapest description, but which always gave immediate and universal pleasure. The same rule holds
good in dress. As in every apartment, so in every
toilet, there should be one ground tone or dominant
color, which should rule all the others, and there
should be a general style of idea to which everything
should be subjected.

"We may illustrate the effect of this principle in a
very familiar case. It is generally conceded that the
majority of women look better in mourning than they
do in their ordinary apparel ; a comparatively plain
person looks almost handsome in simple black. Now
why is this? Simply because mourning requires a
severe uniformity of color and idea, and forbids the
display of that variety of colors and objects which go
to make up the ordinary female costume, and which
very few women have such skill in using as to produce really beautiful effects.

"Very similar results have been attained by the
Quaker costume, which, in spite of the quaint severity
of the forms to which it adhered, has always had a
remarkable degree of becomingness, because of its
restriction to a few simple colors and to the absence
of distracting ornament.

"But the same effect which is produced in mourning or the Quaker costume may be preserved in a
style of dress admitting color and ornamentation. A

dress may have the richest fulness of color, and still the tints may be so chastened and subdued as to produce the impression of a severe simplicity. Suppose, for example, a golden-haired blonde chooses for the ground-tone of her toilet a deep shade of purple, such as affords a good background for the hair and complexion. The larger draperies of the costume being of this color, the bonnet may be of a lighter shade of the same, ornamented with lilac hyacinths, shading insensibly towards rose-color. The effect of such a costume is simple, even though there be much ornament, because it is ornament artistically disposed towards a general result.

"A dark shade of green being chosen as the ground-tone of a dress, the whole costume may, in like manner, be worked up through lighter and brighter shades of green, in which rose-colored flowers may appear with the same impression of simple appropriateness that is made by the pink blossom over the green leaves of a rose. There have been times in France when the study of color produced artistic effects in costume worthy of attention, and resulted in styles of dress of real beauty. But the present corrupted state of morals there has introduced a corrupt taste in dress; and it is worthy of thought that the decline of moral purity in society is often marked oy the deterioration of the sense of artistic beauty.

Corrupt and dissipated social epochs produce corrupt styles of architecture and corrupt styles of drawing and painting, as might easily be illustrated by the history of art. When the leaders of society have blunted their finer perceptions by dissipation and immorality, they are incapable of feeling the beauties which come from delicate concords and truly artistic combinations. They verge towards barbarism, and require things that are strange, odd, dazzling, and peculiar to captivate their jaded senses. Such we take to be the condition of Parisian society now. The tone of it is given by women who are essentially impudent and vulgar, who override and overrule, by the mere brute force of opulence and luxury, women of finer natures and moral tone. The court of France is a court of adventurers, of *parvenus;* and the palaces, the toilets, the equipage, the entertainments, of the mistresses outshine those of the lawful wives. Hence comes a style of dress which is in itself vulgar, ostentatious, pretentious, without simplicity, without unity, seeking to dazzle by strange combinations and daring contrasts.

"Now, when the fashions emanating from such a state of society come to our country, where it has been too much the habit to put on and wear, without dispute and without inquiry, any or everything that France sends, the results produced are often things to make one wonder. A respectable man, sitting quietly in church or other public assembly, may be pardoned sometimes for indulging a silent sense of the ridiculous in the contemplation of the forest of bonnets which surround him, as he humbly asks himself the question, Were these meant to cover the head, to defend it, or to ornament it? and if they are intended for any of these purposes, how?

"I confess, to me nothing is so surprising as the sort of things which well-bred women serenely wear on their heads with the idea that they are ornaments. On my right hand sits a good-looking girl with a thing on her head which seems to consist mostly of bunches of grass, straws, with a confusion of lace, in which sits a draggled bird, looking as if the cat had had him before the lady. In front of her sits another, who has a glittering confusion of beads swinging hither and thither from a jaunty little structure of black and red velvet. An anxious-looking matron appears under the high eaves of a bonnet with a gigantic crimson rose crushed down into a mass of tangled hair. She is *ornamented !* she has no doubt about it.

"The fact is, that a style of dress which allows the use of everything in heaven above or earth beneath requires more taste and skill in disposition than falls to the lot of most of the female sex to make it even tolerable. In consequence, the flowers, fruits, grass, hay, straw, oats, butterflies, beads, birds, tinsel, streamers, jinglers, lace, bugles, crape, which seem to be appointed to form a covering for the female head, very often appear in combinations so singular, and the results, taken in connection with all the rest of the costume, are such, that we really think the people who usually assemble in a Quaker meeting-house are, with their entire absence of ornament, more becomingly attired than the majority of our public audiences. For if one considers his own impression after having seen an assemblage of women dressed in Quaker costume, he will find it to be, not of a confusion of twinkling finery, but of many fair, sweet *faces*, of charming, nice-looking *women*, and not of articles of dress. Now this shows that the severe dress, after all, has better answered the true purpose of dress, in setting forth the *woman*, than our modern costume, where the woman is but one item in a flying mass of colors and forms, all of which distract attention from the faces they are supposed to adorn. The dress of the Philadelphian ladies has always been celebrated for its elegance of effect, from the fact, probably, that the early Quaker parentage of the city formed the eye and the taste of its women for uniform and simple styles of color, and for purity and chastity of lines. The most perfect toilets that have ever been achieved in America have probably been those of the class familiarly called the gay Quakers, — children of Quaker families, who, while abandoning the strict rules of the sect, yet retain their modest and severe reticence, relying on richness of material, and soft, harmonious coloring, rather than striking and dazzling ornament.

"The next source of beauty in dress is the impression of truthfulness and reality. It is a well-known principle of the fine arts, in all their branches, that all shams and mere pretences are to be rejected, — a truth which Ruskin has shown with the full lustre of his many-colored prose-poetry. As stucco pretending to be marble, and graining pretending to be wood, are in false taste in building, so false jewelry and cheap fineries of every kind are in bad taste ; so also is powder instead of natural complexion, false hair instead of real, and flesh-painting of every description. I have even the hardihood to think and assert, in the presence of a generation whereof not one woman in twenty wears her own hair, that the simple, short-cropped locks of Rosa Bonheur are in a more beautiful style of hair-dressing than the most elaborate edifice of curls, rats, and waterfalls that is erected on any fair head now-a-days."

"O Mr. Crowfield! you hit us all now," cried several voices.

"I know it, girls, — I know it. I admit that you

are all looking very pretty; but I do maintain that you are none of you doing yourselves justice, and that Nature, if you would only follow her, would do better for you than all these elaborations. A short crop of your own hair, that you could brush out in ten min· utes every morning, would have a more real, healthy beauty than the elaborate structures which cost you hours of time, and give you the headache besides. I speak of the short crop, — to put the case at the very lowest figure, — for many of you have lovely hair of different lengths, and susceptible of a variety of arrangements, if you did not suppose yourself obliged to build after a foreign pattern, instead of following out the intentions of the great Artist who made you.

"Is it necessary absolutely that every woman and girl should look exactly like every other one? There are women whom Nature makes with wavy or curly hair : let them follow her. There are those whom she makes with soft and smooth locks, and with whom crinkling and craping is only a sham. They look very pretty with it, to be sure; but, after all, is there but one style of beauty? and might they not look prettier in cultivating the style which Nature seemed to have intended for them?

"As to the floods of false jewelry, glass beads, and tinsel finery which seem to be sweeping over the toilet

of our women, I must protest that they are vulgariz
ing the taste, and having a seriously bad effect on the
delicacy of artistic perception. It is almost impossible to manage such material and give any kind of
idea of neatness or purity ; for the least wear takes
away their newness. And of all disreputable things,
tumbled, rumpled, and tousled finery is the most disreputable. A simple white muslin, that can come
fresh from the laundry every week, is, in point of
real taste, worth any amount of spangled tissues. A
plain straw bonnet, with only a ribbon across it, is in
reality in better taste than rubbishy birds or butterflies,
or tinsel ornaments.

"Finally, girls, don't dress at haphazard ; for dress,
so far from being a matter of small consequence, is in
reality one of the fine arts, — so far from trivial, that
each country ought to have a style of its own, and
each individual such a liberty of modification of the
general fashion as suits and befits her person, her age,
her position in life, and the kind of character she
wishes to maintain.

"The only motive in toilet which seems to have
obtained much as yet among young girls is the very
vague impulse to look 'stylish,' — a desire which must
answer for more vulgar dressing than one would wish
to see. If girls would rise above this, and desire to
express by their dress the attributes of true ladyhood,

Q

nicety of eye, fastidious neatness, purity of taste, truthfulness, and sincerity of nature, they might form, each one for herself, a style having its own individual beauty, incapable of ever becoming common and vulgar.

" A truly trained taste and eye would enable a lady to select from the permitted forms of fashion such as might be modified to her purposes, always remembering that simplicity is safe, that to attempt little, and succeed, is better than to attempt a great deal, and fail.

" And now, girls, I will finish by reciting to you the lines old Ben Jonson addressed to the pretty girls of his time, which form an appropriate ending to my remarks.

> ' Still to be dressed
> As you were going to a feast ;
> Still to be powdered, still perfumed ;
> Lady, it is to be presumed,
> Though art's hid causes are not found,
> All is not sweet, all is not sound.
>
> ' Give me a look, give me a face,
> That makes simplicity a grace, —
> Robes loosely flowing, hair as free :
> Such sweet neglect more taketh me
> Than all the adulteries of art,
> That strike my eyes, but not my heart.' "

XI.

THE CATHEDRAL.

" I AM going to build a cathedral one of these days," said I to my wife, as I sat looking at the slant line of light made by the afternoon sun on our picture of the Cathedral of Milan.

" That picture is one of the most poetic things you have among your house ornaments," said Rudolph. " Its original is the world's chief beauty, — a tribute to religion such as Art never gave before and never can again, — as much before the Pantheon, as the Alps, with their virgin snows and glittering pinnacles, are above all temples made with hands. Say what you will, those Middle Ages that you call Dark had a glory of faith that never will be seen in our days of cotton-mills and Manchester prints. Where will you marshal such an army of saints as stands in yonder white-marble forest, visibly transfigured and glorified in that celestial Italian air? Saintship belonged to the mediæval Church; the heroism of religion has died with it."

"That's just like one of your assertions, Rudolph,' said I. "You might as well say that Nature has never made any flowers since Linnæus shut up his herbarium. We have no statues and pictures of modern saints, but saints themselves, thank God, have never been wanting. 'As it was in the begin ning, is now, and ever shall be — '"

"But what about your cathedral?" said my wife.

"O yes! — my cathedral, yes. When my stocks in cloud-land rise, I'll build a cathedral larger than Milan's; and the men, but more particularly the *women*, thereon, shall be those who have done even more than St. Paul tells of in the saints of old, who 'sub dued kingdoms, wrought righteousness, quenched the violence of fire, escaped the edge of the sword, out of weakness were made strong, waxed valiant in fight, turned to flight the armies of the aliens.' I am not now thinking of Florence Nightingale, nor of the host of women who have been walking worthily in her footsteps, but of nameless saints of more retired and private state, — domestic saints, who have tended children not their own through whooping-cough and measles, and borne the unruly whims of fretful inva- lids, — stocking-darning, shirt-making saints, — saints who wore no visible garment of hair-cloth, bound themselves with no belts of spikes and nails, yet in their inmost souls were marked and seared with the red cross of a life-long self-sacrifice, — saints for whom the mystical terms *self-annihilation* and *self-crucifixion* had a real and tangible meaning, all the stronger because their daily death was marked by no outward sign. No mystical rites consecrated them; no organ-music burst forth in solemn rapture to welcome them; no habit of their order proclaimed to themselves and the world that they were the elect of Christ, the brides of another life: but small eating cares, daily prosaic duties, the petty friction of all the littleness and all the inglorious annoyances of every day, were as dust that hid the beauty and grandeur of their calling even from themselves; they walked unknown even to their households, unknown even to their own souls; but when the Lord comes to build his New Jerusalem, we shall find many a white stone with a new name thereon, and the record of deeds and words which only He that seeth in secret knows. Many a humble soul will be amazed to find that the seed it sowed in such weakness, in the dust of daily life, has blossomed into immortal flowers under the eye of the Lord.

"When I build my cathedral, *that* woman," I said, pointing to a small painting by the fire, "shall be among the first of my saints. You see her there, in an every-day dress-cap with a mortal thread-lace border, and with a very ordinary worked collar, fastened by a visible and terrestrial breastpin. There is no nimbus around her head, no sign of the cross upon her breast; her hands are clasped on no crucifix or rosary. Her clear, keen, hazel eye looks as if it could sparkle with mirthfulness, as in fact it could; there are in it both the subtile flash of wit and the subdued light of humor; and though the whole face smiles, it has yet a certain decisive firmness that speaks the soul immutable in good. That woman shall be the first saint in my cathedral, and her name shall be recorded as Saint Esther. What makes saintliness in my view, as distinguished from ordinary goodness, is a certain quality of magnanimity and greatness of soul that brings life within the circle of the heroic. To be really great in little things, to be truly noble and heroic in the insipid details of everyday life, is a virtue so rare as to be worthy of canonization, — and this virtue was hers. New England Puritanism must be credited with the making of many such women. Severe as was her discipline, and harsh as seems now her rule, we have yet to see whether women will be born of modern systems of tolerance and indulgence equal to those grand ones of the olden times whose places now know them no more. The inconceivable austerity and solemnity with which Puritanism invested this mortal life, the awful grandeur of the themes which it made household words, the sublimity of the issues which it hung upon the commonest acts of our earthly existence, created characters of more than Roman strength and greatness ; and the good men and women of Puritan training excelled the saints of the Middle Ages, as a soul fully developed intellectually, educated to closest thought, and exercised in reasoning, is superior to a soul great merely through impulse and sentiment.

"My earliest recollections of Aunt Esther, for so our saint was known, were of a bright-faced, cheerful, witty, quick-moving little middle-aged person, who came into our house like a good fairy whenever there was a call of sickness or trouble. If an accident happened in the great roistering family of eight or ten children, (and when was not something happening to some of us ?) and we were shut up in a sick-room, then duly as daylight came the quick step and cheerful face of Aunt Esther, — not solemn and lugubrious like so many sick-room nurses, but with a never-failing flow of wit and story that could beguile even the most doleful into laughing at their own afflictions. I remember how a fit of the quinsy — most tedious of all sicknesses to an active child — was gilded and glorified into quite a *fête* by my having Aunt Esther all to myself for two whole days, with nothing to do but amuse me. She charmed me into smiling at the very pangs which had made me weep before, and of which she described her own experiences in a manner to make me think that, after all, the quinsy was something with an amusing side to it. Her knowledge of all sorts of medicines, gargles, and alleviatives, her perfect familiarity with every canon and law of good nursing and tending, was something that could only have come from long experience in those good old New England days when there were no nurses recognized as a class in the land, but when watching and the care of the sick were among those offices of Christian life which the families of a neighborhood reciprocally rendered each other. Even from early youth she had obeyed a special vocation as sister of charity in many a sick-room, and, with the usual keen intelligence of New England, had widened her powers of doing good by the reading of medical and physiological works. Her legends of nursing in those days of long typhus-fever and other formidable and protracted forms of disease were to our ears quite wonderful, and we regarded her as a sort of patron saint of the sick-room. She seemed always so cheerful, so bright, and so devoted, that it never occurred to us youngsters to doubt that she enjoyed, above all things, being with us, waiting on us all day, watching over us by night, telling us stories, and answering, in her lively and always amusing and instructive way, tha' incessant fire of questions with which a child persecutes a grown person.

" Sometimes, as a reward of goodness, we were allowed to visit her in her own room, a neat little parlor in the neighborhood, whose windows looked down a hillside on one hand, under the boughs of an apple orchard, where daisies and clover and bobolinks always abounded in summer time, and, on the other, faced the street, with a green yard flanked by one or two shady elms between them and the street. No nun's cell was ever neater, no bee's cell ever more compactly and carefully arranged ; and to us, familiar with the confusion of a great family of little ones, there was something always inviting about its stillness, its perfect order, and the air of thoughtful repose that breathed over it. She lived there in perfect independence, doing, as it was her delight to do, every office of life for herself. She was her own cook, her own parlor and chamber maid, her own laundress ; and very faultless the cooking, washing, ironing, and care of her premises were. A slice of Aunt Esther's gingerbread, one of Aunt Esther's cookies, had, we all believed, certain magical properties such as belonged to no other mortal mixture. Even a handful of walnuts that were brought from the depths of her mysterious closet had virtues in our eyes such as no other walnuts could approach. The little shelf of books that hung suspended by cords against her wall was sacred in our regard ; the volumes were like no other

12

books; and we supposed that she derived from them those stores of knowledge on all subjects which she unconsciously dispensed among us, — for she was always telling us something of metals, or minerals, or gems, or plants, or animals, which awakened our curiosity, stimulated our inquiries, and, above all, led us to wonder where she had learned it all. Even the slight restrictions which her neat habits imposed on our breezy and turbulent natures seemed all quite graceful and becoming. It was right, in our eyes, to cleanse our shoes on scraper and mat with extra diligence, and then to place a couple of chips under the heels of our boots when we essayed to dry our feet at her spotless hearth. We marvelled to see our own faces reflected in a thousand smiles and winks from her bright brass andirons, — such andirons we thought were seen on earth in no other place, — and a pair of radiant brass candlesticks, that illustrated the mantel-piece, were viewed with no less respect.

" Aunt Esther's cat was a model for all cats, — so sleek, so intelligent, so decorous and well-trained, always occupying exactly her own cushion by the fire, and never transgressing in one iota the proprieties belonging to a cat of good breeding. She shared our affections with her mistress, and we were allowed as a great favor and privilege, now and then, to hold the favorite on our knees, and stroke her satin coat to a smoother gloss.

" But it was not for cats alone that she had attractions. She was in sympathy and fellowship with everything that moved and lived ; knew every bird and beast with a friendly acquaintanceship. The squirrels that inhabited the trees in the front-yard were won in time by her blandishments to come and perch on her window-sills, and thence, by trains of nuts adroitly laid, to disport themselves on the shining cherry tea-table that stood between the windows ; and we youngsters used to sit entranced with delight as they gambolled and waved their feathery tails in frolicsome security, eating rations of gingerbread and bits of seed-cake with as good a relish as any child among us.

" The habits, the rights, the wrongs, the wants, and the sufferings of the animal creation formed the subject of many an interesting conversation with her ; and we boys, with the natural male instinct of hunting, trapping, and pursuing, were often made to pause in our career, remembering her pleas for the dumb things which could not speak for themselves.

" Her little hermitage was the favorite resort of numerous friends. Many of the young girls who attended the village academy made her acquaintance, and nothing delighted her more than that they should come there and read to her the books they were studying, when her superior and wide information enabled her to light up and explain much that was not clear to the immature students.

"In her shady retirement, too, she was a sort of Egeria to certain men of genius, who came to read to her their writings, to consult her in their arguments, and to discuss with her the literature and politics of the day, — through all which her mind moved with an equal step, yet with a sprightliness and vivacity peculiarly feminine.

"Her memory was remarkably retentive, not only of the contents of books, but of all that great outlying fund of anecdote and story which the quaint and earnest New England life always supplied. There were pictures of peculiar characters, legends of true events stranger than romance, all stored in the cabinets of her mind ; and these came from her lips with the greater force because the precision of her memory enabled her to authenticate them with name, date, and circumstances of vivid reality. From that shadowy line of incidents which marks the twilight boundary between the spiritual world and the present life she drew legends of peculiar clearness, but invested with the mysterious charm which always dwells in that uncertain region ; and the shrewd flash of her eye, and the keen, bright smile with which she answered the wondering question, 'What *do* you suppose it was ?' or, 'What could it have been ?' showed how evenly rationalism in her mind kept pace with romance.

"The retired room in which she thus read, studied, thought, and surveyed from afar the whole world of science and literature, and in which she received friends and entertained children, was perhaps the dearest and freshest spot to her in the world. There came a time, however, when the neat little independent establishment was given up, and she went to associate herself with two of her nieces in keeping house for a boarding-school of young girls. Here her lively manners and her gracious interest in the young made her a universal favorite, though the cares she assumed broke in upon those habits of solitude and study which formed her delight. From the day that she surrendered this independency of hers, she had never, for more than a score of years, a home of her own, but filled the trying position of an accessory in the home of others. Leaving the boarding-school, she became the helper of an invalid wife and mother in the early nursing and rearing of a family of young children, — an office which leaves no privacy and no leisure. Her bed was always shared with some little one; her territories were exposed to the constant inroads of little pattering feet, and all the various sicknesses and ailments of delicate childhood made absorbing drafts upon her time.

"After a while she left New England with the brother to whose family she devoted herself. The failing health of the wife and mother left more and more the charge of all things in her hands ; servants were poor, and all the appliances of living had the rawness and inconvenience which in those days attended Western life. It became her fate to supply all other people's defects and deficiencies. Wherever a hand failed, there must her hand be. Whenever a foot faltered, she must step into the ranks. She was the one who thought for and cared for and toiled for all, yet made never a claim that any one should care for her.

"It was not till late in my life that I became acquainted with the deep interior sacrifice, the constant self-abnegation, which all her life involved. She was born with a strong, vehement, impulsive nature, — a nature both proud and sensitive, — a nature whose tastes were passions, whose likings and whose aversions were of the most intense and positive character. Devoted as she always seemed to the mere practical and material, she had naturally a deep romance and enthusiasm of temperament which exceeded all that can be written in novels. It was chiefly owing to this that a home and a central affection of her own were never hers. In her early days of attractiveness, none who would have sought her could meet the high requirements of her ideality ; she never saw her hero, — and so never married. Family cares, the tending of young children, she often confessed, were peculiarly irksome to her. She had the head of a student, a passionate love for the world of books. A Protestant convent, where she might devote herself without interruption to study, was her ideal of happiness. She had, too, the keenest appreciation of poetry, of music, of painting, and of natural scenery. Her enjoyment in any of these things was intensely vivid whenever, by chance, a stray sunbeam of the kind darted across the dusty path of her life ; yet in all these her life was a constant repression. The eagerness with which she would listen to any account from those more fortunate ones who had known these things, showed how ardent a passion was constantly held in check. A short time before her death, talking with a friend who had visited Switzerland, she said, with great feeling : ‘ All my life my desire to visit the beautiful places of this earth has been so intense, that I cannot but hope that after my death I shall be permitted to go and look at them.’

"The completeness of her self-discipline may be gathered from the fact, that no child could ever be brought to believe she had not a natural fondness for children, or that she found the care of them burdensome. It was easy to see that she had naturally all those particular habits, those minute pertinacities in respect to her daily movements and the arrangement of all her belongings, which would make the meddling, intrusive demands of infancy and childhood peculiarly hard for her to meet. Yet never was there a pair of toddling feet that did not make free with Aunt Esther's room, never a curly head that did not look up, in confiding assurance of a welcome smile, to her bright eyes. The inconsiderate and never-ceasing requirements of children and invalids never drew from her other than a cheerful response ; and to my mind there is more saintship in this than in the private wearing of any number of hair-cloth shirts or belts lined with spikes.

"In a large family of careless, noisy children there will be constant losing of thimbles and needles and scissors ; but Aunt Esther was always ready, without reproach, to help the careless and the luckless. Her things, so well kept and so treasured, she was willing to lend, with many a caution and injunction it is true, but also with a relish of right good-will. And, to do us justice, we generally felt the sacredness of the trust, and were more careful of her things than of our own. If a shade of sewing-silk were wanting, or a choice button, or a bit of braid or tape, Aunt Esther cheerfully volunteered something from her well-kept stores, not regarding the trouble she made herself in

seeking the key, unlocking the drawer, and searching
out in bag or parcel just the treasure demanded.
Never was more perfect precision, or more perfect
readiness to accommodate others.

"Her little income, scarcely reaching a hundred
dollars yearly, was disposed of with a generosity
worthy a fortune. One tenth was sacredly devoted
to charity, and a still further sum laid by every year
for presents to friends. No Christmas or New Year
ever came round that Aunt Esther, out of this very
tiny fund, did not find something for children and
servants. Her gifts were trifling in value, but well
timed, — a ball of thread-wax, a paper of pins, a
pincushion, — something generally so well chosen as
to show that she had been running over our needs,
and noting what to give. She was no less gracious
as receiver than as giver. The little articles that we
made for her, or the small presents that we could buy
out of our childish resources, she always declared
were exactly what she needed ; and she delighted us
by the care she took of them and the value she set
upon them.

"Her income was a source of the greatest pleasure
to her, as maintaining an independence without which
she could not have been happy. Though she constantly gave, to every family in which she lived, services which no money could repay, it would have

been the greatest trial to her not to be able to provide for herself. Her dress, always that of a true gentlewoman, — refined, quiet, and neat, — was bought from this restricted sum, and her small travelling expenses were paid out of it. She abhorred anything false or flashy: her caps were trimmed with *real* thread-lace, and her silk dresses were of the best quality, perfectly well made and kept; and, after all, a little sum always remained over in her hands for unforeseen exigencies.

"This love of independence was one of the strongest features of her life, and we often playfully told her that her only form of selfishness was the monopoly of saintship, — that she who gave so much was not willing to allow others to give to her, — that she who made herself servant of all was not willing to allow others to serve her.

"Among the trials of her life must be reckoned much ill-health; borne, however, with such heroic patience that it was not easy to say when the hand of pain was laid upon her. She inherited, too, a tendency to depression of spirits, which at times increased to a morbid and distressing gloom. Few knew or suspected these sufferings, so completely had she learned to suppress every outward manifestation that might interfere with the happiness of others. In her hours of depression she resolutely forbore to sadden the lives of those around her with her own melancholy, and often her darkest moods were so lighted up and adorned with an outside show of wit and humor, that those who had known her intimately were astonished to hear that she had ever been subject to depression.

"Her truthfulness of nature amounted almost to superstition. From her promise once given she felt no change of purpose could absolve her ; and therefore rarely would she give it absolutely, for she *could not* alter the thing that had gone forth from her lips. Our belief in the certainty of her fulfilling her word was like our belief in the immutability of the laws of nature. Whoever asked her got of her the absolute truth on every subject, and, when she had no good thing to say, her silence was often truly awful. When anything mean or ungenerous was brought to her knowledge, she would close her lips resolutely ; but the flash in her eyes showed what she would speak were speech permitted. In her last days she spoke to a friend of what she had suffered from the strength of her personal antipathies. 'I thank God,' she said, 'that I believe at last I have overcome all that too, and that there has not been, for some years, any human being toward whom I have felt a movement of dislike.'

"The last year of her life was a constant discipline

of unceasing pain, borne with that fortitude which could make her an entertaining and interesting companion even while the sweat of mortal agony was starting from her brow. Her own room she kept as a last asylum, to which she would silently retreat when the torture became too intense for the repression of society, and there alone, with closed doors, she wrestled with her agony. The stubborn independence of her nature took refuge in this final fastness, and she prayed only that she might go down to death with the full ability to steady herself all the way, needing the help of no other hand.

"The ultimate struggle of earthly feeling came when this proud self-reliance was forced to give way, and she was obliged to leave herself helpless in the hands of others. 'God requires that I should give up my last form of self-will,' she said ; 'now I have resigned *this*, perhaps he will let me go home.'

"In a good old age, Death, the friend, came and opened the door of this mortal state, and a great soul, that had served a long apprenticeship to little things, went forth into the joy of its Lord ; a life of self-sacrifice and self-abnegation passed into a life of endless rest."

"But," said Rudolph, "I rebel at this life of self-abnegation and self-sacrifice. I do not think it the duty of noble women, who have beautiful natures and enlarged and cultivated tastes, to make themselves the slaves of the sick-room and nursery."

" Such was not the teaching of our New England faith," said I. " Absolute unselfishness, — the death of self, — such were its teachings, and such as Esther's the characters it made. ' Do the duty nearest thee,' was the only message it gave to ' women with a mission '; and from duty to duty, from one self-denial to another, they rose to a majesty of moral strength impossible to any form of mere self-indulgence. It is of souls thus sculptured and chiselled by self-denial and self-discipline that the living temple of the perfect hereafter is to be built. The pain of the discipline is short, but the glory of the fruition is eternal."

XII.

THE NEW YEAR.

/

[1865.]

HERE comes the First of January, Eighteen Hundred and Sixty-Five, and we are all settled comfortably into our winter places, with our winter surroundings and belongings; all cracks and openings are calked and listed, the double windows are in, the furnace dragon in the cellar is ruddy and in good liking, sending up his warming respirations through every pipe and register in the house; and yet, though an artificial summer reigns everywhere, like bees, we have our swarming-place, — in my library. There is my chimney-corner, and my table permanently established on one side of the hearth; and each of the female genus has, so to speak, pitched her own winter-tent within sight of the blaze of my camp-fire. I discerned to-day that Jennie had surreptitiously appropriated one of the drawers of my study-table to knitting-needles and worsted; and wicker work-baskets and stands of various heights and sizes seem to be planted here and there for permanence among the bookcases. The canary-bird has a sunny window, and the plants spread out their leaves and unfold their blossoms as if there were no ice and snow in the street, and Rover makes a hearth-rug of himself in winking satisfaction in front of my fire, except when Jennie is taken with a fit of discipline, when he beats a retreat, and secretes himself under my table.

Peaceable, ah, how peaceable, home and quiet and warmth in winter! And how, when we hear the wind whistle, we think of you, O our brave brothers, our saviors and defenders, who for our sake have no home but the muddy camp, the hard pillow of the barrack, the weary march, the uncertain fare, — you, the rank and file, the thousand unnoticed ones, who have left warm fires, dear wives, loving little children, without even the hope of glory or fame, — without even the hope of doing anything remarkable or perceptible for the cause you love, — resigned only to fill the ditch or bridge the chasm over which your country shall walk to peace and joy! Good men and true, brave unknown hearts, we salute you, and feel that we, in our soft peace and security, are not worthy of you! When we think of you, our simple comforts seem luxuries all too good for us, who give so little when you give all!

But there are others to whom from our bright homes,

our cheerful firesides, we would fain say a word, if we dared.

Think of a mother receiving a letter with such a passage as this in it! It is extracted from one we have just seen, written by a private in the army of Sheridan, describing the death of a private. " He fell instantly, gave a peculiar smile and look, and then closed his eyes. We laid him down gently at the foot of a large tree. I crossed his hands over his breast, closed his eyelids down, but the smile was still on his face. I wrapt him in his tent, spread my pocket-handkerchief over his face, wrote his name on a piece of paper, and pinned it on his breast, and there we left him : we could not find pick or shovel to dig a grave." There it is ! — a history that is multiplying itself by hundreds daily, the substance of what has come to so many homes, and must come to so many more before the great price of our ransom is paid !

What can we say to you, in those many, many homes where the light has gone out forever ? — you, O fathers, mothers, wives, sisters, haunted by a name that has ceased to be spoken on earth, — you, for whom there is no more news from the camp, no more reading of lists, no more tracing of maps, no more letters, but only a blank, dead silence ! The battle· cry goes on, but for you it is passed by ! the victory comes, but, oh, never more to bring him back to you !

your offering to this great cause has been made, and been taken ; you have thrown into it *all* your living, even all that you had, and from henceforth your house is left unto you desolate ! O ye watchers of the cross, ye waiters by the sepulchre, what can be said to you? We could almost extinguish our own home-fires, that seem too bright when we think of your darkness ; the laugh dies on our lip, the lamp burns dim through our tears, and we seem scarcely worthy to speak words of comfort, lest we seem as those who mock a grief they cannot know.

But is there no consolation ? Is it nothing to have had such a treasure to give, and to have given it freely for the noblest cause for which ever battle was set, — for the salvation of your country, for the freedom of all mankind ? Had he died a fruitless death, in the track of common life, blasted by fever, smitten or rent by crushing accident, then might his most precious life seem to be as water spilled upon the ground ; but now it has been given for a cause and a purpose worthy even the anguish of your loss and sacrifice. He has been counted worthy to be numbered with those who stood with precious incense between the living and the dead, that the plague which was consuming us might be stayed. The blood of these young martyrs shall be the seed of the future church of liberty, and from every drop shall spring up flowers of healing. O

widow ! O mother ! blessed among bereaved women '
there remains to you a treasure that belongs not to
those who have lost in any other wise, — the power to
say, " He died for his country." In all the good that
comes of this anguish you shall have a right and share
by virtue of this sacrifice. The joy of freedmen burst-
ing from chains, the glory of a nation new-born, the
assurance of a triumphant future for your country and
the world, — all these become yours by the purchase-
money of that precious blood.

Besides this, there are other treasures that come
through sorrow, and sorrow alone. There are celestial plants of root so long and so deep that the land
must be torn and furrowed, ploughed up from the
very foundation, before they can strike and flourish ;
and when we see how God's plough is driving backward and forward and across this nation, rending,
tearing up tender shoots, and burying soft wild-flowers,
we ask ourselves, What is He going to plant?

Not the first year, nor the second, after the ground
has been broken up, does the purpose of the husband-
man appear. At first we see only what is uprooted
and ploughed in, — the daisy drabbled, and the violet
crushed, — and the first trees planted amid the unsightly furrows stand dumb and disconsolate, irreso-
lute in leaf, and without flower or fruit. Their work
is under the ground. In darkness and silence they

are putting forth long fibres, searching hither and thither under the black soil for the strength that years hence shall burst into bloom and bearing.

What is true of nations is true of individuals. It may seem now winter and desolation with you. Your hearts have been ploughed and harrowed and are now frozen up. There is not a flower left, not a blade of grass, not a bird to sing,— and it is hard to believe that any brighter flowers, any greener herbage, shall spring up than those which have been torn away ; and yet there will. Nature herself teaches you to-day. Out-doors nothing but bare branches and shrouding snow ; and yet you know that there is not a tree that is not patiently holding out at the end of its boughs next year's buds, frozen indeed, but unkilled. The rhododendron and the lilac have their blossoms all ready, wrapped in cere-cloth, waiting in patient faith. Under the frozen ground the crocus and the hyacinth and the tulip hide in their hearts the perfect forms of future flowers. And it is even so with you : your leaf-buds of the future are frozen, but not killed ; the soil of your heart has many flowers under it cold and still now, but they will yet come up and bloom.

The dear old book of comfort tells of no present healing for sorrow. *No* chastening for the present seemeth joyous, but grievous, but *afterwards* it yieldeth peaceable fruits of righteousness. We, as indi viduals, as a nation, need to have faith in that AFTER WARDS. It is sure to come, — sure as spring and summer to follow winter.

There is a certain amount of suffering which must follow the rending of the great cords of life, suffering which is natural and inevitable; it cannot be argued down; it cannot be stilled; it can no more be soothed by any effort of faith and reason than the pain of a fractured limb, or the agony of fire on the living flesh. All that we can do is to brace ourselves to bear it, calling on God, as the martyrs did in the fire, and resigning ourselves to let it burn on. We must be willing to suffer since God so wills. There are just so many waves to go over us, just so many arrows of stinging thought to be shot into our soul, just so many faintings and sinkings and revivings only to suffer again, belonging to and inherent in our portion of sorrow; and there is a work of healing that God has placed in the hands of Time alone.

Time heals all things at last; yet it depends much on us in our suffering, whether time shall send us forth healed, indeed, but maimed and crippled and callous, or whether, looking to the great Physician of sorrows, and coworking with him, we come forth stronger and fairer even for our wounds.

We call ourselves a Christian people, and the pecu-liarity of Christianity is that it is a worship and doctrine of sorrow. The five wounds of Jesus, the instruments of the passion, the cross, the sepulchre, — these are its emblems and watchwords. In thousands of churches, amid gold and gems and altars fragrant with perfume, are seen the crown of thorns, the nails, the spear, the cup of vinegar mingled with gall, the sponge that could not slake that burning death-thirst; and in a voice choked with anguish the Church in many lands and divers tongues prays from age to age, " By thine agony and bloody sweat, by thy cross and passion, by thy precious death and burial ! " — mighty words of comfort, whose meaning reveals itself only to souls fainting in the cold death-sweat of mortal anguish ! They tell all Christians that by uttermost distress alone was the Captain of their salvation made perfect as a Saviour.

Sorrow brings us into the true unity of the Church, — that unity which underlies all external creeds, and unites all hearts that have suffered deeply enough to know that when sorrow is at its utmost there is but one kind of sorrow, and but one remedy. What matter, *in extremis*, whether we be called Romanist, or Protestant, or Greek, or Calvinist?

We suffer, and Christ suffered; we die, and Christ died; he conquered suffering and death, he rose and lives and reigns, — and we shall conquer, rise, live, and reign. The hours on the cross were long, the thirst was bitter, the darkness and horror real, — *but they ended.* After the wail, "My God, why hast thou forsaken me?" came the calm, "It is finished"; pledge to us all that our "It is finished" shall come also.

Christ arose, fresh, joyous, no more to die; and it is written, that, when the disciples were gathered together in fear and sorrow, he stood in the midst of them, and showed unto them his hands and his side; and then were they glad. Already had the healed wounds of Jesus become pledges of consola- tion to innumerable thousands; and those who, like Christ, have suffered the weary struggles, the dim horrors of the cross, — who have lain, like him, cold and chilled in the hopeless sepulchre, — if his spirit wakes them to life, shall come forth with healing power for others who have suffered and are suffering.

Count the good and beautiful ministrations that have been wrought in this world of need and labor, and how many of them have been wrought by hands wounded and scarred, by hearts that had scarcely ceased to bleed!

How many priests of consolation is God now or- daining by the fiery imposition of sorrow! how many Sisters of the Bleeding Heart, Daughters of Mercy Sisters of Charity, are receiving their first vocation ir tears and blood!

The report of every battle strikes into some home ; and heads fall low, and hearts are shattered, and only God sees the joy that is set before them, and that shall come out of their sorrow. He sees our morning at the same moment that He sees our night, — sees us comforted, healed, risen to a higher life, at the same moment that He sees us crushed and broken in the dust ; and so, though tenderer than we, He bears our great sorrows for the joy that is set before us.

After the Napoleonic wars had desolated Europe, the country was, like all countries after war, full of shattered households, of widows and orphans and homeless wanderers. A nobleman of Silesia, the Baron von Kottwitz, who had lost his wife and all his family in the reverses and sorrows of the times, found himself alone in the world, which looked more dreary and miserable through the multiplying lenses of his own tears. But he was one of those whose heart had been quickened in its death anguish by the resurrection voice of Christ ; and he came forth to life and comfort. He bravely resolved to do all that one man could to lessen the great sum of misery. He sold his estates in Silesia, bought in Berlin a large building that had been used as barracks for the soldiers, and, fitting it up in plain, commodious apartments, formed there a great family-establishment, into which he received the wrecks and fragments of families that had been broken up by the war, — orphan children, widowed and helpless women, decrepit old people, disabled soldiers. These he made his family, and constituted himself their father and chief. He abode with them, and cared for them as a parent. He had schools for the children ; the more advanced he put to trades and employments ; he set up a hospital for the sick ; and for all he had the priestly ministrations of his own Christ-like heart. The celebrated Professor Tholuck, one of the most learned men of modern Germany, was an early *protégé* of the old Baron's, who, discerning his talents, put him in the way of a liberal education. In his earlier years, like many others of the young who play with life, ignorant of its needs, Tholuck piqued himself on a lordly scepticism with regard to the commonly received Christianity, and even wrote an essay to prove the superiority of the Mohammedan to the Christian religion. In speaking of his conversion, he says, — "What moved me was no argument, nor any spoken reproof, but simply that divine image of the old Baron walking before my soul. That life was an argument always present to me, and which I never could answer ; and so I became a Christian." In the life of this man we see the victory over sorrow. How many with means like his, when desolated by like bereavements, have lain coldly and idly gazing on the miseries of life, and weaving around themselves icy tissues of doubt and despair, — doubting the being of a God, doubting the reality of a Providence, doubting the divine love, imbittered and rebellious against the power which they could not resist, yet to which they would not submit! In such a chill heart-freeze lies the danger of sorrow. And it is a mortal danger. It is a torpor that must be resisted, as the man in the whirling snows must bestir himself, or he will perish. The apathy of melancholy must be broken by an effort of religion and duty. The stagnant blood must be made to flow by active work, and the cold hand warmed by clasping the hands outstretched towards it in sympathy or supplication. One orphan child taken in, to be fed, clothed, and nurtured, may save a heart from freezing to death : and God knows this war is making but too many orphans !

It is easy to subscribe to an orphan asylum, and go on in one's despair and loneliness. Such ministries may do good to the children who are thereby saved from the street, but they impart little warmth and comfort to the giver. One destitute child housed, taught, cared for, and tended personally, will bring more solace to a suffering heart than a dozen main tained in an asylum. Not that the child will prob ably prove an angel, or even an uncommonly interesting mortal. It is a prosaic work, this bringing-up of children, and there can be little rosewater in it. The child may not appreciate what is done for him, may not be particularly grateful, may have disagreeable faults, and continue to have them after much pains on your part to eradicate them, — and yet it is a fact, that to redeem one human being from destitution and ruin, even in some homely every-day course of ministrations, is one of the best possible tonics and alteratives to a sick and wounded spirit.

But this is not the only avenue to beneficence which the war opens. We need but name the service of hospitals, the care and education of the freedmen, — for these are charities that have long been before the eyes of the community, and have employed thousands of busy hands : thousands of sick and dying beds to tend, a race to be educated, civilized, and Christianized, surely were work enough for one age ; and yet this is not all. War shatters everything, and it is hard to say what in society will not need rebuilding and binding up and strengthening anew. Not the least of the evils of war are the vices which a great army engenders wherever it moves, — vices peculiar to military life, as others are peculiar to peace. The poor soldier perils for us not merely his body, but his soul. He leads a life of harassing and exhausting toil and privation, of violent strain on the nervous energies, alternating with sudden collapse, creating a craving for stimulants, and endangering the formation of fatal habits. What furies and harpies are those that follow the army, and that seek out the soldier in his tent, far from home, mother, wife, and sister, tired, disheartened, and tempt him to forget his troubles in a momentary exhilaration, that burns only to chill and to destroy! Evil angels are always active and indefatigable, and there must be good angels enlisted to face them; and here is employment for the slack hand of grief. Ah, we have known mothers bereft of sons in this war, who have seemed at once to open wide their hearts, and to become mothers to every brave soldier in the field. They have lived only to work, — and in place of one lost, their sons have been counted by thousands.

And not least of all the fields for exertion and Christian charity opened by this war is that presented by womanhood. The war is abstracting from the community its protecting and sheltering elements, and leaving the helpless and dependent in vast disproportion. For years to come, the average of lone women will be largely increased; and the demand, always great, for some means by which they may provide for themselves, in the rude jostle of the world, will become more urgent and imperative.

Will any one sit pining away in inert grief, when two streets off are the midnight dance-houses, where girls of twelve, thirteen, and fourteen are being lured into the way of swift destruction? How many of these are daughters of soldiers who have given their hearts' blood for us and our liberties!

Two noble women of the Society of Friends have lately been taking the gauge of suffering and misery in our land, visiting the hospitals at every accessible point, pausing in our great cities, and going in their purity to those midnight orgies where mere children are being trained for a life of vice and infamy. They have talked with these poor bewildered souls, entangled in toils as terrible and inexorable as those of the slave-market, and many of whom are frightened and distressed at the life they are beginning to lead, and earnestly looking for the means of escape. In the judgment of these holy women, at least one third of those with whom they have talked are children so recently entrapped, and so capable of reformation, that there would be the greatest hope in efforts for their salvation. While such things are to be done in our land, is there any reason why any one should die of grief? One soul redeemed will do more to lift the burden of sorrow than all the blandishments and diversions of art, all the alleviations of luxury, all the sympathy of friends.

In the Roman Catholic Church there is an order of women called the Sisters of the Good Shepherd.

who have renounced the world to devote themselves, their talents and property, entirely to the work of seeking out and saving the fallen of their own sex; and the wonders worked by their self-denying love on the hearts and lives of even the most depraved are credible only to those who know that the Good Shepherd Himself ever lives and works with such spirits engaged in such a work. A similar order of women exists in New York, under the direction of the Episcopal Church, in connection with St. Luke's Hospital; and another in England, who tend the "House of Mercy" of Clewer.

Such benevolent associations offer objects of interest to that class which most needs something to fill the void made by bereavement. The wounds of grief are less apt to find a cure in that rank of life where the sufferer has wealth and leisure. The *poor* widow, whose husband was her all, *must* break the paralysis of grief. The hard necessities of life are her physicians; they send her out to unwelcome, yet friendly toil, which, hard as it seems, has yet its healing power. But the sufferer surrounded by the appliances of wealth and luxury may long indulge the baleful apathy, and remain in the damp shadows of the valley of death till strength and health are irrecoverably lost. How Christ-like is the thought of a woman, graceful, elegant, cultivated, refined, whose voice has been

trained to melody, whose fingers can make sweet har-
mony with every touch, whose pencil and whose needle can awake the beautiful creations of art, devoting
all these powers to the work of charming back to the
sheepfold those wandering and bewildered lambs
whom the Good Shepherd still calls his own! Jenny
Lind, once, when she sang at a concert for destitute
children, exclaimed in her enthusiasm, "Is it not
beautiful that I can sing so?" And so may not every
woman feel, when her graces and accomplishments
draw the wanderer, and charm away evil demons, and
soothe the sore and sickened spirit, and make the
Christian fold more attractive than the dizzy gardens
of false pleasure?

In such associations, and others of kindred nature,
how many of the stricken and bereaved women of our
country might find at once a home and an object in
life! Motherless hearts might be made glad in a
better and higher motherhood; and the stock of
earthly life that seemed cut off at the root, and dead
past recovery, may be grafted upon with a shoot from
the tree of life which is in the Paradise of God.

So the beginning of this eventful 1865, which finds
us still treading the wine-press of our great conflict,
should bring with it a serene and solemn hope, a joy
such as those had with whom in the midst of the fiery
furnace there walked one like unto the Son of God.

The great affliction that has come upon our country is so evidently the purifying chastening of a Father, rather than the avenging anger of a Destroyer, that all hearts may submit themselves in a solemn and holy calm still to bear the burning that shall make us clean from dross and bring us forth to a higher national life. Never, in the whole course of our history, have such teachings of the pure abstract Right been so commended and forced upon us by Providence. Never have public men been so constrained to humble themselves before God, and to acknowledge that there is a Judge that ruleth in the earth. Verily his inquisition for blood has been strict and awful; and for every stricken household of the poor and lowly hundreds of households of the oppressor have been scattered. The land where the family of the slave was first annihilated, and the negro, with all the loves and hopes of a man, was proclaimed to be a beast to be bred and sold in market with the horse and the swine, — that land, with its fair name, Virginia, has been made a desolation so signal, so wonderful, that the blindest passer-by cannot but ask for what sin so awful a doom has been meted out. The prophetic visions of Nat Turner, who saw the leaves prop blood and the land darkened, have been fulfilled. The work of justice which he predicted is being executed to the uttermost.

But when this strange work of judgment and justice is consummated, when our country, through a thousand battles and ten thousands of precious deaths, shall have come forth from this long agony, redeemed and regenerated, then God himself shall return and dwell with us, and the Lord God shall wipe away all tears from all faces, and the rebuke of his people shall he utterly take away.

XIII.

THE NOBLE ARMY OF MARTYRS.

WHEN the first number of the Chimney-Corner appeared, the snow lay white on the ground, the buds on the trees were closed and frozen, and beneath the hard frost-bound soil lay buried the last year's flower-roots, waiting for a resurrection.

So in our hearts it was winter, — a winter of patient suffering and expectancy, — a winter of suppressed sobs, of inward bleedings, — a cold, choked, compressed anguish of endurance, for how long and how much God only could tell us.

The first paper of the Chimney-Corner, as was most meet and fitting, was given to those homes made sacred and venerable by the cross of martyrdom, — by the chrism of a great sorrow. That Chimney-Corner made bright by home firelight seemed a fitting place for a solemn act of reverent sympathy for the homes by whose darkness our homes had been preserved bright, by whose emptiness our homes had

13 *

been kept full, by whose losses our homes had been enriched ; and so we ventured with trembling to utter these words of sympathy and cheer to those whom God had chosen to this great sacrifice of sorrow.

The winter months passed with silent footsteps, spring returned, and the sun, with ever-waxing power, unsealed the snowy sepulchre of buds and leaves, — birds. reappeared, brooks were unchained, flowers filled every desolate dell with blossoms and perfume. And with returning spring, in like manner, the chill frost of our fears and of our dangers melted before the breath of the Lord. The great war, which lay like a mountain of ice upon our hearts, suddenly dissolved and was gone. The fears of the past were as a dream when one awaketh, and now we scarce realize our deliverance. A thousand hopes are springing up everywhere, like spring-flowers in the forest. All is hopefulness, all is bewildering joy.

But this our joy has been ordained to be changed into a wail of sorrow. The kind hard hand, that held the helm so steadily in the desperate tossings of the storm, has been stricken down just as we entered port, — the fatherly heart that bore all our sorrows can take no earthly part in our joys. His were the cares, the watchings, the toils, the agonies, of a nation ·n mortal struggle ; and God, looking down, was so well pleased with his humble faithfulness, his patient continuance in well-doing, that earthly rewards and honors seemed all too poor for him, so he reached down and took him to immortal glories. " Well done, good and faithful servant, enter thou into the joy of thy Lord ! "

Henceforth the place of Abraham Lincoln is first among that noble army of martyrs who have given their blood to the cause of human freedom. The eyes are yet too dim with tears that would seek calmly to trace out his place in history. He has been a marvel and a phenomenon among statesmen, a new kind of ruler in the earth. There has been something even unearthly about his extreme unselfishness, his utter want of personal ambition, personal self-valuation, personal feeling.

The most unsparing criticism, denunciation, and ridicule never moved him to a single bitter expression, never seemed to awaken in him a single bitter thought. The most exultant hour of party victory brought no exultation to him ; he accepted power not as an honor, but as a responsibility ; and when, after a severe struggle, that power came a second time into his hands, there was something preternatural in the calmness of his acceptance of it. The first impulse seemed to be a disclaimer of all triumph over the party that had strained their utmost to push him from nis seat, and then a sober girding up of his loins to go on with the work to which he was appointed. His last inaugural was characterized by a tone so peculiarly solemn and free from earthly passion, that it seems to us now, who look back on it in the light of what has followed, as if his soul had already parted from earthly things, and felt the powers of the world to come. It was not the formal state-paper of the chief of a party in an hour of victory, so much as the solemn soliloquy of a great soul reviewing its course under a vast responsibility, and appealing from all earthly judgments to the tribunal of Infinite Justice. It was the solemn clearing of his soul for the great sacrament of Death, and the words that he quoted in it with such thrilling power were those of the adoring spirits that veil their faces before the throne : " Just and true are thy ways, thou King of saints ! "

Among the rich treasures which this bitter struggle has brought to our country, not the least is the moral wealth which has come to us in the memory of our martyrs. Thousands of men, women, and children too, in this great conflict, have " endured tortures, not accepting deliverance," counting not their lives dear unto them in the holy cause ; and they have done this as understandingly and thoughtfully as the first Christians who sealed their witness with their blood.

Let us in our hour of deliverance and victory record the solemn vow, that our right hand shall forget her cunning before we forget them and their sufferings, — that our tongue shall cleave to the roof of our mouth if we remember them not above our chief joy.

Least suffering among that noble band were those who laid down their lives on the battle-field, to whom was given a brief and speedy passage to the victor's meed. The mourners who mourn for such as these must give place to another and more august band, who have sounded lower deeps of anguish, and drained bitterer drops out of our great cup of trembling.

The narrative of the lingering tortures, indignities, and sufferings of our soldiers in Rebel prisons has been something so harrowing that we have not dared to dwell upon it. We have been helplessly dumb before it, and have turned away our eyes from what we could not relieve, and therefore could not endure to look upon. But now, when the nation is called to strike the great and solemn balance of justice, and to decide measures of final retribution, it behooves us all that we should at least watch with our brethren for one hour, and take into our account what they have been made to suffer for us.

Sterne said he could realize the miseries of captivity only by setting before him the image of a miserable captive with hollow cheek and wasted eye, notch-

ing upon a stick, day after day, the weary record of
the flight of time. So we can form a more vivid
picture of the sufferings of our martyrs from one
simple story than from any general description ; and
therefore we will speak right on, and tell one story
which might stand as a specimen of what has been
done and suffered by thousands.

In the town of Andover, Massachusetts, a boy of
sixteen, named Walter Raymond, enlisted among our
volunteers. He was under the prescribed age, but
his eager zeal led him to follow the footsteps of an
elder brother who had already enlisted; and the father of the boy, though these two were all the sons
he had, instead of availing himself of his legal right to
withdraw him, indorsed the act in the following letter
addressed to his Captain : —

"ANDOVER, MASS., August 15, 1862.

"CAPTAIN HUNT, — My eldest son has enlisted in
your company. I send you his younger brother.
He is, and always has been, in perfect health, of
more than the ordinary power of endurance, honest,
truthful, and courageous. I doubt not you will find
him on trial all you can ask, except his age, and that
I am sorry to say is only sixteen; yet if our country
needs his service, take him.

"Your obedient servant,

"SAMUEL RAYMOND."

The boy went forth to real service, and to successive battles at Kingston, at Whitehall, and at Goldsborough ; and in all did his duty bravely and faithfully. He met the temptations and dangers of a soldier's life with the pure-hearted firmness of a Christian child, neither afraid nor ashamed to remember his baptismal vows, his Sunday-school teachings, and his mother's wishes.

He had passed his promise to his mother against drinking and smoking, and held it with a simple, childlike steadiness. When in the midst of malarious swamps, physicians and officers advised the use of tobacco. The boy writes to his mother : " A great many have begun to smoke, but I shall not do it without your permission, though I think it does a great deal of good."

In his leisure hours, he was found in his tent reading ; and before battle he prepared his soul with the beautiful psalms and collects for the day, as appointed by his church, and writes with simplicity to his friends, —

" I prayed God that he would watch over me, and if I fell, receive my soul in heaven ; and I also prayed that I might not forget the cause I was fighting for, and turn my back in fear."

After nine months' service, he returned with a soldier's experience, though with a frame weakened by sickness in a malarious region. But no sooner did health and strength return than he again enlisted, in the Massachusetts cavalry service, and passed many months of constant activity and adventure, being in some severe skirmishes and battles with that portion of Sheridan's troops who approached nearest to Richmond, getting within a mile and a half of the city. At the close of this raid, so hard had been the service, that only thirty horses were left out of seventy-four in his company, and Walter and two others were the sole survivors among eight who occupied the same tent.

On the 16th of August, Walter was taken prisoner in a skirmish; and from the time that this news reached his parents, until the 18th of the following March, they could ascertain nothing of his fate. A general exchange of prisoners having been then effected, they learned that he had died on Christmas Day in Salisbury Prison, of hardship and privation.

What these hardships were is, alas! easy to be known from those too well-authenticated accounts published by our government of the treatment experienced by our soldiers in the Rebel prisons.

Robbed of clothing, of money, of the soldier's best friend, his sheltering blanket, — herded in shivering nakedness on the bare ground, — deprived of every implement by which men of energy and spirit had soon bettered their lot, — forbidden to cut in adjacent forests branches for shelter, or fuel to cook their coarse food, — fed on a pint of corn-and-cob-meal per day, with some slight addition of molasses or rancid meat, — denied all mental resources, all letters from home, all writing to friends, — these men were cut off from the land of the living while yet they lived, — they were made to dwell in darkness as those that have been long dead.

By such slow, lingering tortures, — such weary, wasting anguish and sickness of body and soul, — it was the infernal policy of the Rebel government either to wring from them an abjuration of their country, or by slow and steady draining away of the vital forces to render them forever unfit to serve in her armies.

Walter's constitution bore four months of this usage, when death came to his release. A fellow-sufferer, who was with him in his last hours, brought the account to his parents.

Through all his terrible privations, even the lingering pains of slow starvation, Walter preserved his steady simplicity, his faith in God, and unswerving fidelity to the cause for which he was suffering.

When the Rebels had kept the prisoners fasting for days, and then brought in delicacies to tempt their appetite, hoping thereby to induce them to desert

T

their flag, he only answered, "I would rather be carried out in that dead-cart!"

When told by some that he must steal from his fellow-sufferers, as many did, in order to relieve the pangs of hunger, he answered, "No, I was not brought up to that!" And so when his weakened system would no longer receive the cob-meal which was his principal allowance, he set his face calmly towards death.

He grew gradually weaker and weaker and fainter and fainter, and at last disease of the lungs set in, and it became apparent that the end was at hand.

On Christmas Day, while thousands among us were bowing in our garlanded churches or surrounding festive tables, this young martyr lay on the cold, damp ground, watched over by his destitute friends, who sought to soothe his last hours with such scanty comforts as their utter poverty afforded, — raising his head on the block of wood which was his only pillow, and moistening his brow and lips with water, while his life ebbed slowly away, until about two o'clock, when he suddenly roused himself, stretched out his hand, and, drawing to him his dearest friend among those around him, said, in a strong, clear voice : —

"I am going to die. Go tell my father I am ready to die, for I die for God and my country," — and looking up with a triumphant smile, he passed to the reward of the faithful.

And now, men and brethren, if this story were a single one, it were worthy to be had in remembrance; but Walter Raymond is not the only noble-hearted boy or man that has been slowly tortured and starved and done to death, by the fiendish policy of Jefferson Davis and Robert Edmund Lee.

No, — wherever this simple history shall be read, there will arise hundreds of men and women who will testify, "Just so died my son!" "So died my brother!" "So died my husband!" "So died my father!"

The numbers who have died in these lingering tortures are to be counted, not by hundreds, or even by thousands, but by tens of thousands.

And is there to be no retribution for a cruelty so vast, so aggravated, so cowardly and base? And if there is retribution, on whose head should it fall? Shall we seize and hang the poor, ignorant, stupid, imbruted semi-barbarians who were set as jailers to keep these hells of torment and inflict these insults and cruelties? or shall we punish the educated, intelligent chiefs who were the head and brain of the iniquity?

If General Lee had been determined *not* to have prisoners starved or abused, does any one doubt that he could have prevented these things? Nobody doubts it. His raiment is red with the blood of his helpless captives.   Does any one doubt that Jefferson Davis, living in ease and luxury in Richmond, knew that men were dying by inches in filth and squalor and privation in the Libby Prison, within bowshot of his own door?   Nobody doubts it.   It was his will, his deliberate policy, thus to destroy those who fell into his hands.   The chief of a so-called Confederacy, who could calmly consider among his official documents incendiary plots for the secret destruction of ships, hotels, and cities full of peaceable people, is a chief well worthy to preside over such cruelties ; but his only just title is President of Assassins, and the whole civilized world should make common cause against such a miscreant.

There has been, on both sides of the water, much weak, ill-advised talk of mercy and magnanimity to be extended to these men, whose crimes have produced a misery so vast and incalculable.   The wretches who have tortured the weak and the helpless, who have secretly plotted to supplement, by dastardly schemes of murder and arson, that strength which failed them in fair fight, have been commiserated as brave generals and unfortunate patriots, and efforts are made to place them within the comities of war.

It is no feeling of personal vengeance, but a sense of the eternal fitness of things, that makes us rejoice, when criminals, who have so outraged every sentiment of humanity, are arrested and arraigned and awarded due retribution at the bar of their country's justice. There are crimes against God and human nature which it is treason alike to God and man not to punish; and such have been the crimes of the traitors who were banded together in Richmond.

If there be those whose hearts lean to pity, we can show them where all the pity of their hearts may be better bestowed than in deploring the woes of assassins. Let them think of the thousands of fathers, mothers, wives, sisters, whose lives will be forever haunted with memories of the slow tortures in which their best and bravest were done to death.

The sufferings of those brave men are ended. Nearly a hundred thousand are sleeping in those sad, nameless graves, — and may their rest be sweet! " There the wicked cease from troubling, there the weary are at rest. There the prisoners rest together; they hear not the voice of the oppressor." But, O ye who have pity to spare, spare it for the broken-hearted friends, who, to life's end, will suffer over and over all that their dear ones endured. Pity the mothers who hear their sons' faint calls in dreams, who in many a weary night-watch see them pining and wasting, and yearn with a life-long, unappeasable yearning to have been able to soothe those forsaken, lonely death-beds. Oh, man or woman, if you have pity to spare, spend it not on Lee or Davis, — spend it on their victims, on the thousands of living hearts which these men of sin have doomed to an anguish that will end only with life !

Blessed are the mothers whose sons passed in battle, — a quick, a painless, a glorious death ! Blessed in comparison, — yet we weep for them. We rise up and give place at sight of their mourning-garments. We reverence the sanctity of their sorrow. But before this other sorrow we are dumb in awful silence. We find no words with which to console such grief. We feel that our peace, our liberties, have been bought at a fearful price, when we think of the sufferings of our martyred soldiers. Let us think of them. It was for *us* they bore hunger and cold and nakedness. They might have had food and raiment and comforts, if they would have deserted our cause, — and they did not. Cut off from all communication with home or friends or brethren, — dragging on the weary months, apparently forgotten, — still they would not yield, they would not fight against us ; and so for us at last they died.

What return can we make them ? Peace has come, and we take up all our blessings restored and brightened ; but if we look, we shall see on every blessing a bloody cross.

When three brave men broke through the ranks of

the enemy, to bring to King David a draught from the home-well, for which he longed, the generous-hearted prince would not drink it, but poured it out as an offering before the Lord; for he said, " Is not this the blood of the men that went in jeopardy of their lives?"

Thousands of noble hearts have been slowly consumed to secure to us the blessings we are rejoicing in.

We owe a duty to these our martyrs, — the only one we can pay.

In every place, honored by such a history and example, let a monument be raised at the public expense, on which shall be inscribed the names of those who died for their country, and the manner of their death.

Such monuments will educate our young men in heroic virtue, and keep alive to future ages the flame of patriotism. And thus, too, to the aching heart of bereaved love shall be given the only consolation of which its sorrows admit, in the reverence which is paid to its lost loved ones.

THE END.